# SMALL GROUPS WITH PURPOSE

## *How to Create Healthy Communities*

### Steve Gladen

a division of Baker Publishing Group
Grand Rapids, Michigan

© 2011 by Steve Gladen

Published by Baker Books
a division of Baker Publishing Group
P.O. Box 6287, Grand Rapids, MI 49516-6287
www.bakerbooks.com

Printed in the United States of America

Library of Congress Cataloging-in-Publication Data
Gladen, Steve, 1960–
    Small groups with purpose : how to create healthy communities / Steve Gladen.
        p.    cm.
    Includes bibliographical references (p.    ).
    ISBN 978-0-8010-1379-9 (cloth)
    1. Church group work. 2. Small groups—Religious aspects—Christianity.
I. Title.
BV652.2.G485 2011
253'.7—dc22                                                                2010050761

11   12   13   14   15   16   17        7   6   5   4   3   2   1

To the small group point people around the world. You are my heroes! You slug it out day in and day out to build health in your church. Yours is the hidden ministry most people never see, but never forget this: God sees it!

# Contents

# Foreword

Small groups are the heart of Saddleback Church. They are the source of our church's health and growth. Small groups are the center of our discipleship, the structure of our ministry, the launch pad of our evangelism, the enrichment of our worship, and the network of our fellowship.

In 1980, when I was a twenty-five-year-old following God's leading to Southern California to begin a new church, there was so much I *didn't* know. I didn't know how Kay and I would feed ourselves and our four-month-old baby. I didn't know where we'd live, let alone where we would hold our first worship service. One thing I did know, however, was that this church would be built on relationships.

The first person I invited to attend was the very first person I met—the Realtor who found us a condo to rent. Two weeks later we held our first Bible study in the living room of that condo. There were seven of us. Like most churches, we began as a small group. Today, thirty years later, Saddleback members meet weekly in more than 3,500 small groups. From the start, groups have been our strategy for assimilation and discipleship.

Christlike churches have one thing in common: they find a way to meet the needs of the people God has placed in their ministry areas. People are hungry for love, purpose, and life transformation, and I know of no better structure than a small group where this happens naturally and personally. That's why churches must grow larger and smaller at the same time—larger through evangelism and smaller through fellowship structures.

Over the years, our styles and methods have changed to meet the changing needs of our community. But what has not changed is our gospel message of God's grace and the universal human need for relationships. Even in the perfect Garden of Eden, God said, "It is not good for man to be alone." Groups meet that longing for belonging.

I always tell new attenders at Saddleback, "You will not really feel connected to Saddleback until you join and participate in a small group." Of course, people know this in a larger church, but I believe it is also true in smaller churches. It is impossible to feel truly connected to a crowd, even if that crowd is only fifty people. Crowds are great for worship, but they simply cannot provide personal attention, encouragement, prayer support, a listening ear, and accountability. I need those things. So do the people of your church. So do you.

In *The Purpose Driven Church*, I wrote, "The key to a healthy church, just like a healthy body, is balance." Balance is also the key to a healthy small group ministry. And in this long-awaited book, Saddleback's brilliant pastor of small groups shares the biblical strategy, the secrets, the failures, and the lessons behind the remarkable growth of our small groups. Saddleback may possibly be the only church in America that consistently has thousands more people attend weekly Bible study in groups than attend our weekend services. So much of that is due to the genius of Steve Gladen, a pastor with a passionate heart for Jesus and his body.

Today our world is facing five global giants: spiritual emptiness, egocentric leadership, extreme poverty, pandemic diseases, and lack of education. The public and private sectors have failed to eradicate these crippling problems. The only organization large enough and powerful enough to take on these problems is the global network of Christian churches that exists in every corner of the world—specifically, the small groups of people within those churches. These small groups can work to *Promote* reconciliation, *Equip* servant leaders, *Assist* the poor, *Care* for the sick, and *Educate* the next generation. We call it the P.E.A.C.E. plan, and we invite you to join us!

Imagine an army of people composed of small groups from your church spreading across the world to do just that. In the past five years, Saddleback Church has sent out over 14,000 of our members to *every nation* of the world—195 nations—through the P.E.A.C.E. plan. How were we able to mobilize such an army? Two words: small groups!

If you are not harnessing and directing the latent energy of your members for the Great Commission and great commandment, your church will never be the church that God intends, and your people will never reach their God-intended maturity in Christ. So I invite you not just to read this book, but to study it with your leaders and adopt the biblical structures of "temple courts" and "house to house," as the book of Acts repeatedly mentions. It will change your people. It will change your church. It will change your community. It can change the world!

Rick Warren, Saddleback Church

# Acknowledgments

Many thanks to:

The senior pastors who have played a huge role in my life before Saddleback Church: Gene Speich, Paul Currie, George Smith, Charles Blair, Jason Garcia, and Larry DeWitt. Thanks for your role in shaping me for kingdom service.

Rick and Kay Warren, who have poured into me since 1983 without even knowing it. Your constant dedication to ministry, pastoral families, and the health of the church are overwhelming. You are the same on the platform as you are in person. Your sacrifice makes this book possible and the small group ministry of Saddleback Church what it is. I wish everyone could get a glimpse of the pastor I know day in and day out. You are my pastor. Thanks for leading!

Cheryl Shireman, who wrote a critical email that led her to become part of the solution and the right arm of the Small Group Network. Her passion for writing and making sense of senseless thoughts has been the salvation for me and this book. She read my mind and brought this book to life! Cheryl, you are a godsend.

Jeanine Feld, who has lived this journey more than most by being next to me since December 1998, making my ministry more effective for his kingdom. Your unseen hours devoted to Saddleback

Church, the Small Group Conferences, and the Small Group Network are the untold story. Your reward is truly in heaven.

Brett Eastman, who brought me to Saddleback. What started out as a lunch turned into the ride of a lifetime! Thanks for believing in me.

The small group team: Tom Atkins, Jean Bushong, Jennifer Cantwell, Tom Crick, Debbie Eaton, Jeanine Feld, Karen Fera, Kerri Johnson, Wayne Jones, Deanna Kaech, Kenny Luck, Efraim Meulenberg, Helen Mitchell, Todd Olthoff, Tina Pretsch, Chris Reed, Sheila Rowe, Laura Sullivan, Ron Wilbur, Stacey Woodhart, Rick Zeiger, and the secret four who are nevertheless a key part of our team: Dick Whitton, Jim Brewington, Jeffrey Slipp, and Brian Olsen. To the BDTITLE, thanks for the mentoring, ministry, moments, and fun as we figure this out.

The Small Group Network leadership: Ed Applegate, Alastair Bate, Vinnie Cappetta, Jay Daniell, David Hull, Ian Kirk, Mark Mehlig, Michael Moore, Eddie Mosley, Cheryl Shireman, Reid Smith, Jon Weiner, and Ron Youtsey, who cover North America with me, and to the area and local leadership, who make the network strong so that nobody stands alone.

Those who read the manuscript and gave suggestions that made this book better: Carolyn Taketa, Christi Hamilton, Rick Howerton, Reid Smith, Spence Shelton, William Groff, Chip Kelly, Doug Fields, Greig Gladen, Todd Gladen, Nita Bukowski, Dave Alford, Lance Witt, Ben Reed, Adam Workman, Matt Harmer, Chris Dunayski, and Eric Van Alstine.

Rick Howerton and Mike May for their contributions to chapter 15. Thanks for helping me in the Sunday school environment.

The more than 3,500 small group leaders of Saddleback Church who week in and week out shape the destinations of thousands of folks one life at a time.

My small group, who has lived this crazy journey with Lisa and me: Bill and Elaine Crane, John and Janet Hertogh, Gina and Tyra Rikimaru. Our families are forever knit together.

My parents, who took a risk in their fifties to follow Christ and who are waiting for us in heaven—party on! To my brothers Kurt, Greig, Todd, Mark, and my brave sister, Nita; I love life with you and wish geography wasn't between us. Move to Southern California!

Lisa, Erika, and Ethan, whom I would die for and who are the reason I get up in the morning. Lisa, you cheer me on and give me grace. Since 1988 you have believed in me and this book. You sacrifice more than anyone knows; you are the strength behind our marriage, family, and ministry. I love you! Erika and Ethan, you bring a smile and a glimpse into the future. I pray for your growth in the Lord and impact for his kingdom. Live strong for him!

To Jesus Christ, who strengthens me and makes this whole work possible.

# Introduction

## *The Purpose of This Book*

When I came to you, brothers, I did not come with eloquence or superior wisdom as I proclaimed to you the testimony about God. For
I resolved to know nothing while I was with you except Jesus Christ
and him crucified. I came to you in weakness and fear, and with much
trembling. My message and my preaching were not with wise and
persuasive words, but with a demonstration of the Spirit's power, so
that your faith might not rest on men's wisdom, but on God's power.

1 Corinthians 2:1–5

A man's errors are his portals of discovery.

James Joyce

On a daily basis, the small group team at Saddleback Church is in-
undated with questions from small group point people, lead pastors,
and small group leaders. The denominations and locales vary, but the
questions are all centered on one fundamental question: How can I
improve my small group ministry? The callers and emailers look at
Saddleback, a megachurch with over 3,500 adult small groups, and
assume we have all of the answers. Let me say right now that we do
not have all of the answers. I do believe, however, that we have found
some of the answers through both our failures and our successes.

The people who call, email, and come to our Small Group Conferences desire to learn and get answers to their questions. If they are on the
church staff, it is likely they are trying to lead the small group ministry

while also directing a different ministry. They may not be getting paid at all, and even if they are, the money they are making is not commensurate with the hours they are working. Very often they are pouring their hearts into the ministry with little or no support from anyone inside or outside their church. They call, email, or come to workshops and conferences eager to talk to someone—anyone—about small groups.

I talk with them on the phone, through emails, after workshops, or as we meet in the hallway during conferences. In these impromptu meetings, I am unable to give them the full attention they deserve. My answers are shorter than I would like them to be and lack the detail they need. For example, I remember meeting Norma from Missouri on a break from teaching. Her question was a good one, but my time was short. I rushed to answer her, but quite honestly, the answer was *good enough* at best.

This book is my attempt to answer those questions in far greater detail, to throw out a lifeline, and to share with you some of the mistakes I have made and some of the things that I have learned from those mistakes.

This book is organized around the questions I asked in my journey—the same questions I now am asked every week.

What is a healthy and balanced small group?
What does this look like?
Step-by-step, how can I do this?
What does this mean for overall church strategy?

And one more important question that is often unasked:

Do I have what it takes?

I am a hands-on kind of a guy. I don't want to just read information; I want to begin processing it and applying it to my situation. In fact, in my office there is a whiteboard with the maxim: "Vision without implementation is hallucination!" I want to help you begin the implementation process, which is why there is a section entitled "Questions" at the end of each chapter.

In this format of the written word, I will be able to talk with you without being in a hurry to move to another workshop or take another call. I will be here at your convenience. So grab a cup of coffee (Venti with cream and three Splendas for me), sit down, and let's begin.

# What Is a
# Healthy and
# Balanced
# Small Group?

# 1

# My Story

## *And What It Has Taught Me about Ministry*

He must increase, but I must decrease.

John 3:30 NASB

It's not my ability, but my response to God's ability, that counts.

Corrie Ten Boom

Ministry did not come easily to me. At the point I felt God calling me to ministry, my response was, "God, you have got the wrong person." From that point, it was a seven-year run from God. I did everything I could to avoid going into ministry.

I have mild dyslexia, and when I am thinking quickly, I sometimes mix things up. If I am reading aloud, I sometimes swap words around and try to make sense of it as I go. This didn't make school very easy for me. I remember my sixth grade teacher, Miss Beatenhead (yup, I'm not making that up), getting frustrated with me because I never fully spelled out my name on papers. I would often write "Stev" or "Glade." I remember her asking me in front of the entire class, "How will you make it if you can't even spell your name?" I sank down in my chair and wondered the same.

Being raised Catholic, however, my fear of God was greater than my fear of failure, and I enrolled in Evangel College (now Evangel University) in Springfield, Missouri, even though I didn't exactly feel like college material. As a condition of acceptance, I had to take high school–level English classes during my first year. Not exactly an ego builder.

In addition, although my parents probably could have afforded to pay for my schooling, they believed I would appreciate my education more if I worked for it. At the time, I didn't care for that philosophy, but looking back, I can see they were right. During high school I worked part-time for a cable television company, so when it came time to find employment in Springfield, I looked for a job in that field. By God's providence, a new company called TeleCable was starting up. The general manager, Jerry Rutherford, was kind enough to hire me and allowed me to work a flexible schedule around my classes.

After four years in Springfield, I completed my BA in biblical studies with minors in Greek and philosophy. It was a tough four years, and I had to spend more time than most reading and studying. Social life was almost nonexistent. I had also just completed four years with a small company that started with just a few employees and had grown into a large company, and I actually liked my job. I had become comfortable in it, the pay was good, and the people I worked with had become family. Instead of going home during my last two summers, I actually stayed in Springfield and worked full-time to make extra money for school.

As graduation neared, an internal struggle began to develop. Should I stay in Springfield and continue working at the cable company or move on to graduate school? The possibility of working in a church didn't even cross my mind. I couldn't imagine how church ministry could be part of my future.

One day after work I ran into the general manager of the company, Jerry. I realize now this brief meeting was a God encounter that changed my course in life. I had previously shared my struggle with Jerry, and on that day he told me I was welcome to stay at TeleCable and he would never fire me. But then he went on to say he didn't believe God's plan was for me to stay. He felt my destiny was to finish what God started, and if a church wasn't the next step, I should honor God and continue on to graduate school. Jerry was a godly and wise man, and like a word from heaven, his words went straight to my heart. Everything I knew, everything that was comfortable and familiar, I was about to lose.

I applied to Fuller Theological Seminary, was accepted, and attended the Pasadena campus. With my previous experience, I quickly landed a job with another cable company. Unlike Jerry at TeleCable, however, my new boss did everything he could to make my life miserable. Looking back, I think it was God's way of pushing me away from the comfort of working with a cable company and toward staying focused on graduate school and the possibility of working in a church. My schedule was tough, and it seemed as though every hour was spent attending class, working, studying, or sleeping. On the positive side, California felt like home. It was odd, since I was raised in Ohio and had just spent four years in Missouri, but when I moved to California in 1982, I felt as though I had come home.

I took morning classes or night classes and worked for the cable company in the afternoon. I felt as though I had a foot in both worlds. Most of the graduate students were already involved in ministry, but I remained outside that circle. I doubted myself. I felt inadequate. But I stayed. I struggled. I obeyed. Mostly I tried not to think about it.

I remember my guidance counselor at Fuller saying, "You're good. You try hard. But you can't graduate with a master's degree until you actually work at a church."

After a year and a half I decided to quit the job at the cable company. I remember wondering what I was going to do without the security of that job and no other possibilities before me. Shortly after, however, using a connection through my friend Doug Schmidt, God opened a door and gave me the opportunity to work as an intern for Pastor Paul Currie, who retired within a year. I had no church background and limited connections, so the very fact that I was accepted as an intern under such conditions was a miracle in itself. Although I wondered how God would provide, I felt at peace knowing my career was in his hands.

Somewhere during this time I came across 1 Corinthians 2:1–5:

When I came to you, brothers, I did not come with eloquence or superior wisdom as I proclaimed to you the testimony about God. For I resolved to know nothing while I was with you except Jesus Christ and him crucified. I came to you in weakness and fear, and with much trembling. My message and my preaching were not with wise and persuasive words, but with a demonstration of the Spirit's power, so that your faith might not rest on men's wisdom, but on God's power.

I felt as though God gave those verses directly to me when I needed them the most. I suddenly realized I was not alone in feeling inadequate; many before me had felt the same way. In fact, all I had to do was trust God, and his power would see me through whatever challenges were ahead. Of course that didn't erase all of my self-doubt and fear, but I knew that I didn't need wise and eloquent words and I was confident that God, through the Holy Spirit, would provide for my shortcomings. It was nothing short of life-changing. I remember telling my mom, and she told me she had known I was destined for ministry from the time I accepted Christ. She was only waiting for me to catch on!

*It is interesting to note that Jesus didn't pick the Who's Who in Jerusalem.*

When Christ called the original disciples, what was the first requirement? *Follow me.* That is a very low bar. It is interesting to note that Jesus didn't pick the Who's Who in Jerusalem—the people with the most influence or the ones with the most biblical education (which by the way would have been the Pharisees and Sadducees). Instead, he picked the most obedient. Christ can use you in your weakness and fear if you will only obey and follow him. As I read this verse (Matt. 4:19) for what seemed like the first time, I realized God could use me too.

We are all on the same team, and if we work together we can accomplish a great deal. Since my Fuller days I have worked on staff for five churches of five different denominations—small churches (just north of one hundred members), medium-size churches, and megachurches. If the focus is on Jesus, amazing things can happen regardless of size and denomination.

You will never have all of the answers. But you don't have to have all of the answers; you just need to obey. If I had given in to my self-doubt and fear, I would be comfortably working in a cable company today.

## Questions

These questions are intended to spark your thinking. Don't feel you have to answer all of them at one sitting. After reflecting on them, mark one in every chapter that particularly stands out to you. Then when you have finished reading the book, take some time and go back to the questions you marked and consider them from your new perspective. Have fun.

What are some of the things you are afraid of losing when you think about reorganizing or starting your small group ministry?

_____

_____

_____

As you look at your life story, where do you see the hand of God?

_____

_____

_____

Are there any new areas where you feel God might be leading you now?

_____

_____

_____

Is there anything you are clinging to that might be a hindrance to God moving you into a new direction?

_____

_____

_____

# 2

## The Saddleback Difference

### The Ten Foundations of Saddleback's Small Group Ministry

> For we walk by faith, not by sight.
>
> 2 Corinthians 5:7 KJV

> The key issue for groups in the twenty-first century will be health, not growth.
>
> Rick Warren

Our church is located in Orange County, California, and has over 20,000 people in attendance on an average weekend. Your church probably does not fit this description. God has a specific plan for Saddleback, and he has a specific plan for your church too. In this book I will share a lot about what has worked for us at Saddleback; it's up to you to decide what will work for you in your ministry context.

## Method versus Message

All too often people go to a conference and then try to implement in their home church the strategies that succeeded at another church. Very often their efforts fail. The fact that the strategies cannot be transferred to a church in a different setting, however, may have nothing to do with the merits of the strategy. Methods may or may not transfer. Principles, however, will always transfer. Principles are based on truth; God's Word is the truth. It is not the truth only in certain locations; it is the truth in every location. "If God's knowledge is complete and perfectly true, then truth itself cannot change; it remains the same for every time and place in creation; it is absolute."[1] Methods are merely what works in a given situation, a given culture.

*The methods must continually change but the message must never change.*

The *methods* must continually change but the *message* must never change. For example, some of Christ's last words were, "Go make disciples." As Christians, our responsibility is to make disciples, but *how* we make disciples has changed drastically over the years. For example, people may use television, the Internet, DVDs, CDs, MP3s, books, movies, social media, and so forth. The change reflects new technologies, our culture, and the times in which we live, but the message stays the same.

## All Types of Churches to Reach All Types of People

A very small church may be very healthy; a very large church may be very unhealthy. This is also true of small group ministries—size is not indicative of health. When we have shared what works for us at Saddleback, sometimes the response is, "Sure, that works for you. You are a huge church with lots of resources." The thing people forget, though, is that Saddleback also started out as a small church. It began as seven people meeting in Rick and Kay Warren's living room. It is hard to get much smaller than that. Adhering to sound principles enabled Saddleback to grow not only in size but also in health.

Your church may never be over a hundred members in size. It may never have more than two groups. That is not necessarily an indication of poor health. You may be limited by the demographic of the people you are trying to reach or simply by smaller population in general. For example, if you are working with a church whose members are primarily older people who are accustomed to attending Sunday school, they may be very hesitant to ever join a small group. That doesn't mean, however, that your Sunday school groups can't be healthy. We firmly believe the key issue for small groups in the twenty-first century is health, not numerical growth.

## Saddleback Small Groups

I am often asked about Saddleback's small group strategy. How were we able to go from a small group of seven people meeting in Rick Warren's living room to a church of over 3,500 adult small groups (and still growing)? There's no quick or easy answer. Since our small group strategy has a lot in common with those of other churches, I can't point to a specific key to our success. One thing remains constant at Saddleback Church, and that is our *message*. Meanwhile, our methods are always evolving and are subject to change. I can point to ten foundational principles we use that evolved as we sought to follow God's leading in reaching and connecting people into life-changing, healthy small groups. These ten principles not only have formed our strategy through the years but also serve as a funnel through which all our present-day decisions are made. Each one of them was developed in the *laboratory* of Saddleback Church since its inception in 1980.

*In order for us to master change, our paradigm must switch from what we will lose to what we will gain.*

As you read about these principles and then continue through this book, please keep an open mind. Don't assume that something will not work because your church doesn't resemble Saddleback Church. Be open to all possibilities and avenues of thinking. So often we focus on what we will lose because of change. In order for us to master change, our paradigm must switch from what we will lose to what we will gain.

### 1. Bold Faith, Not Cautious Planning

From the beginning, when Saddleback Church was just a dream in the heart of twenty-six-year-old Rick Warren, bold faith has always taken precedence over cautious planning. "Very little of Saddleback's ministry was preplanned," Rick writes in his book *The Purpose Driven*

*Church*.[2] Instead, Rick followed the leading of the Holy Spirit and quickly responded to circumstances surrounding him. In fact, when he moved his wife, Kay, and their four-month-old baby to Orange County, California, they did not know a single person in the area. He writes that they were full of hope, "but we also arrived with no money, no church building, no members, and no home."[3] Did that make sense? No, not so much. But Rick had faith and was willing to follow the leading of God, even if it did not seem to make sense at the time.

In March of 1980 he stood in a high school gymnasium before the very first congregation of sixty people (most of them unbelievers). Confidently, and almost flat broke, he announced that someday they would be a church of over 20,000 members and they would build a facility on at least fifty acres of land in Orange County, California (some of the most expensive real estate in the United States). He finished by adding, "I stand before you today and state in confident assurance that these dreams will become reality. Why? Because they are inspired by God!"[4]

Today, Saddleback Valley Community Church has an average weekly attendance of over 20,000 people and sits on 120 acres of prime Orange County real estate. Christmas and Easter services average well over 40,000 in attendance. Rick would be the first to tell you the success of Saddleback has been more about faith in following the leading of the Holy Spirit than the careful and strategic planning of a single man.

This bold faith is the kind of faith that enabled David to confront Goliath with a sling and five stones gathered from a stream. It is the kind of faith that gave Abraham the strength to place Isaac on the altar as a sacrifice. This kind of faith now leads Rick Warren to take on the five global giants (spiritual emptiness, corrupt leadership, extreme poverty, pandemic disease, and rampant illiteracy) through the P.E.A.C.E. Plan (*Promote* reconciliation, *Equip* servant leaders, *Assist* the poor, *Care* for the sick, and *Educate* the next generation). This bold faith is foundational to Saddleback and to all we do. If we believe God is leading, the dream is never too big—never impossible.

In the small group ministry it is the same. So often I call Rick Warren the *small group pastor* of Saddleback Church. We have two *delivery systems* at Saddleback—two ways we strategically distribute all five biblical purposes, which we will discuss in the next point. Based on Acts 5:42, they are: (1) temple courts (weekend services) and (2) house to house (small groups). Temple courts should be the mouthpiece of house to house; temple courts and house to house are interwoven and collaborate together for the same cause. If you have a powerful temple courts leader who believes in small groups, your job is much easier.

In each and every phase since 1998, problem solving has never trumped decision making. When we have been at a crossroads in the small group ministry, we follow God's decision and sort the rest out as we go. Many examples run through my head of decisions when bold faith was needed and we were blessed to see God's mighty hand at work in the ministry. In 2007, after a one-week fast, it was clear to me that in order to get to our next goal in small groups set by the church and our team, we needed to take fifty-two part-time, paid positions (paid staff who served as *community leaders* overseeing a group of small group leaders) and re-staff them as volunteer positions. The current structure wasn't broken, but in order to reach our next level, we needed far more community leaders than our budget could afford. Today, as I look back, it would have been easy to leave it the same, but it would not have been right. Over half the paid community leaders (CLs) stayed on as volunteers, and today we have 188 volunteer CLs managing the small group ministry. Taking the ministry to the next level required faith and obedience on the part of everyone involved.

**Figure 2.1**

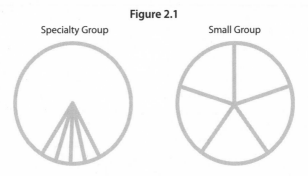

Specialty Group                                    Small Group

### 2. Purpose Driven Groups, Not Special-Interest Groups

In his book *The Purpose Driven Church*, Rick writes, "We don't expect each small group to do the same things; we allow them to specialize."[5] That was in 1995. As time went by, we began to learn more about two groupings of people we have at Saddleback: small groups and specialty groups (see figure 2.1).

Groups of people who meet around special interests or ministries of the church are strategic, but they are not trying to balance the five biblical purposes (fellowship, discipleship, ministry, evangelism, and worship) to create healthy individuals and groups. For example, while our greeters ministry groups are an important and strategic ministry of the church, those groups don't generally focus on the *health* of the individuals and group but on greeting people who come to our campus.

Our small groups, on the other hand, focus on individual and group health and balance, and this book is all about the *small group* side of the church. Of course it doesn't matter whether you call your groups small groups, cell groups, community groups, or some other term; what matters is a healthy small group ministry full of healthy small groups. And we are looking for groups that are *balanced*, which as a verb means "to bring into harmony or proportion."[6] Today at Saddleback we expect every small group to focus on health through balancing the five biblical purposes: fellowship, discipleship, ministry, evangelism, and worship. We call these purpose driven small groups.

We get these five biblical purposes from the Great Commission (Matt. 28:19–20) and the great commandment (Matt. 22:37–40).

Fellowship: "Baptizing them in the name of the Father and of the Son and of the Holy Spirit" (28:19).

Discipleship: "Teaching them to obey everything I have commanded you" (28:20).

Ministry: "Love your neighbor as yourself" (22:39).

Evangelism: "Go and make disciples of all nations" (28:19).

Worship: "Love the Lord your God with all your heart and with all your soul and with all your mind" (22:37).

Rick Warren sums up the Saddleback philosophy in *The Purpose Driven Church*: "These two passages summarize everything we do at Saddleback Church. If an activity or program fulfills one of these commands, we do it. If it doesn't, we don't."[7] Our small group philosophy reflects the philosophy of the overall church. It is not enough for us to think about these purposes in the corporate structure of the church alone. It is not enough for people to be exposed to the five purposes only on weekends. We want them to experience the five biblical purposes in the context of a small group so that ultimately they become part of daily life.

We are far more concerned about *healthy* groups than we are about the *number* of groups. Having many groups or even having a large percentage of our people in groups is not the ultimate goal because it is possible to have a large number of small groups that are not producing fruit or life change.

In their desire to build health in their members, most churches have four delivery systems they use outside the weekend services: (1) Sunday school, (2) small groups, (3) midweek teaching, and (4) Sunday night services. Of course each church needs to come to its own conclusions, but more often than not, I see churches using certain delivery systems just because that is what they have always done. I suggest that rather than beginning with what your church has always done, start by asking yourself what kind of people you are trying to produce. Then begin exploring what delivery system would be best for fulfilling that outcome.

### 3. Effective, Not Perfect

Our small group ministry strives to be effective, not perfect. We never let problem solving get in the way of a decision that must be made. Our biggest strides have been made by pulling the trigger on ideas at the right moment, not by agonizing over every possible scenario that could go wrong. I love Ecclesiastes 11:4, which says, "If you wait for perfect conditions, you'll never get anything done" (TLB). We don't make perfection an idol, and we are not idle waiting for perfect conditions. If you are single and waiting for the perfect conditions to get married, you will always be single. If you are married and waiting for the perfect conditions to have kids, you will never have kids. God wants us to be good stewards of our resources, not roadblocks to his promptings. Sometimes we just overthink it.

*We never let problem solving get in the way of a decision that must be made.*

During a management meeting in the summer of 2002, Pastor Rick spoke to us about *exponential thinking*. In the past we usually launched around 300 groups per year, but that year he challenged us to launch 3,000 groups. In that moment, the campaign strategy was born—a strategy that now has been used successfully by thousands of churches around the world.

I would like to say we had it all figured out from the beginning. But that would be far from the truth. When Pastor Rick first had the idea of the campaign strategy, we were only six weeks away from our fall program launch, so we had a very short time to come up with small group resources. What later came together in a nicely organized kit called 40 Days of Purpose, which we later packaged for outside churches, actually started with us scrambling to get good enough resources to our groups week by week. Could we have made it look better for our own groups? Sure. But we would have missed the wave God wanted us to surf.

### 4. Intentional Focus, Not Flavor of the Day

In order for a small group strategy to be successful, a church must know how it will define success. Everything we do in the small group ministry falls under our vision and mission. Our *vision* is the reason we are here: to see every person, from the core of our church to the ever-growing community, connected in a healthy small group. Our *mission* is what we do: we help spiritual seekers become transformed believers who model purpose driven lives and motivate others to do the same.

Furthermore, our small group vision and mission support the overall purpose of Saddleback Church. I am not suggesting that you adopt our vision and mission, but I am suggesting that you have your own and that they direct your every action. They should keep you focused; they are the compass that shows you true north. In this book I will discuss how you can develop a laser-beam focus that will enable you to be intentional in your strategy and effective in your actions.

If your small group ministry lacks a clear purpose and focus, it will flounder and your small group members will see little value in joining other than fellowship. Too often, small group point people focus more on getting people into small groups than on defining the purpose of the small group ministry. You search for new small group curriculum or creative ways to train your leaders, but the real problem is a lack of focus and purpose. The Bible tells us in Ephesians 5:17, "Therefore do not be foolish, but understand what the Lord's will is." Every church must discover what God's will is for their small group ministry. The small group point person's role is to then fulfill that purpose. I believe my purpose as a small group point person is to see the five biblical purposes lived out in our groups and in the lives of the individuals in those groups.

If someone asked you what your church's plan is for connecting people into small groups, could you articulate it clearly? Better yet, if I went to your church and asked some of your key leaders, could they articulate the strategy? How about the members of your church? Could these people describe the process that people go through from the time they walk in your door as guests in the worship service to the time they are plugged into some kind of small group? Does everyone in your church know the process your church has developed to facilitate placing people into small groups? If you do not have an intentional focus and strategy, a lot of your people will walk in the front door to attend the worship service and then go their own ways to do ministry. Or worse yet, they may slip right out the back door, never to be heard from again.

I have a letter that is a harsh reminder of that fact. The opening line is seared into my mind. "After much prayer and soul searching, this letter is to inform Saddleback of our family's decision to leave as members of the church." The letter was sent directly to Pastor Rick, but my boss and I had also been copied. I had not been on staff long, but it still wounded like a knife to the heart. "We have had virtually no contact with anyone from the church regarding our small group in the five years we have been leading it. We have felt detached from the church as leaders." I had two choices at that point. I could have thought, *I haven't been on staff that long, so this is someone else's problem.* Or I could see this as an example of what happens when we fail to have an intentional strategy to connect and support people and do my best to ensure that it never happened again. I chose the latter, and that letter sat on my desk for years as a reminder. It is now in my conference notebook where I keep all of my notes for my conference lectures. I read from it as part of my presentation to other small group point people. It is still humbling and painful to read, but it is an important part of my journey as a leader and a reminder of what I never want sent to me again!

*If you wait for perfect people to lead your small groups, you'll be waiting until Christ's return.*

### 5. *Leadership Potential, Not Proven Leaders*

If you wait for perfect people to lead your small groups, you'll be waiting until Christ's return. You don't need all-star, supertrained small group leaders to create a successful small group ministry. All you need is people who are willing and obedient. Remember, God doesn't call the equipped; he equips the called. Using biblically solid studies, even a member who is very young in the faith can be a *host* (our term for small group leaders, which will be explained in greater detail in chapters 12 and 13). We get people involved early in leading groups and then help them to develop the required skills *as* they lead.

Prior to coming to Saddleback, my small group strategy was to fully equip leaders through training before actually allowing them to lead. At Saddleback I worked with a team to develop a different strategy. The idea is to give people an entry-level opportunity to lead a small group. They don't have to be seasoned veterans of the faith. They don't have to be experienced leaders. We have made it very simple for people to take a first step into leadership.

This is the model Jesus gave us when he chose twelve ordinary men to be his disciples. His first words of training were *follow me*. "'Come, follow me,' Jesus said, 'and I will make you fishers of men'" (Matt. 4:19). That invitation started a three-year process of on-the-job training that culminated in the disciples being so committed that they were willing to die for the cause. The problem in churches is that we often skip past the *follow me* and scare off leaders by asking them to *come die for me*.

### 6. Simple Systems, Not Complex Structures

I have become convinced that the long-term success of leaders is determined by the support and resources they receive. Right now we have eighteen-, nineteen-, and twenty-year-old men and women who are serving in harm's way around the world. Military commanders would never send these young men and women to the front lines without training, without equipping, without a command and control process, or without supply lines. The commanders try to do everything within their power to set up the soldiers to succeed in the mission they have been given.

Obviously, leading a small group is not the same thing as flying to the Middle East in a military jet. But we are sending our small group leaders out to the front lines of ministry. Ephesians 6:10–20 makes it quite clear that our battle is both spiritual and aggressive. If you are going to ask people in your church to step up and take the risk of leading, shepherding, and giving pastoral care, it is vital to provide resources and support for them.

No matter how good your small group strategy is, though, your growth will be limited unless you have an infrastructure to support it. At

Saddleback we look for small group leaders who are natural in caring for people to begin training for broader leadership roles. We then develop and support them through our Small Group Leadership Development Pathway (this is discussed in detail in chapter 13). This pathway helps them understand the ministry, teaches them how to recognize God's call in their lives, and then trains them in head and heart fundamentals so they can be even more effective in the ministry. The Small Group Leadership Development Pathway provides the support our leaders need by building an infrastructure of volunteer community leaders (leaders of leaders) to develop, guide, and encourage our small group leaders.

Some people believe every small group should receive equal care. At Saddleback, however, we have found that not all groups are equal, so we believe in strategic care, not equal care. Some groups have very mature leadership. Some groups are brand-new. Some are full of baby Christians. Others have been liberally sprinkled with challenging types of people. Of course we love them all, but we shouldn't put the same effort and attention into them all because some will need more and others will need less. We have found that equal care can actually hinder leadership development and health. In subsequent chapters I will explain how we prioritize our groups based on four categories and how this simplified care management will allow your leadership infrastructure to be more effective.

### 7. Churchwide Alignment

Saddleback was the first church to use the campaign strategy— uniting the entire congregation around a single, multiweek DVD study that is executed through the weekend services and small group gatherings. This campaign strategy offers several advantages. One of the most desirable is that it puts the whole church on the same page, since during the duration of the campaign, the entire congregation is moving in the same direction. In the same manner, your staff should all be on the same page and moving in the same direction. Every ministry leader, and eventually every staff member, must buy into the overall vision and mission of your church. Your lead pastor's job is to communicate the value of small groups at every level—to the staff, to the members, and to people visiting your church.

Small groups are not optional at Saddleback. Our job applications clearly state, "If you accept a position on the staff, we expect you to be active in a small group." This book will explain how you can influence not only your staff culture but also your church culture through ministry alignment and making use of all of your avenues of communication.

### 8. Growth by Campaigns, Not Disrupting Community

Small group ministries live in constant tension between fellow-ship and evangelism. We want small group members to develop deep relationships, but we also need to integrate new people into groups. Many churches handle integration of new people by asking existing groups to add new members or to break up and multiply into two or more smaller groups so they can add new members. All too often the result is that group members resent the intrusion, and a frustrated small group point person has to try continually to sell a concept to the small groups that they simply do not buy. We have found that it is better for all concerned to start new groups than for existing groups to multiply.

*Small group ministries live in constant tension between fellowship and evangelism.*

So how do we integrate new people? In short, through campaigns. We have grown to more than 3,500 adult small groups by using campaigns to launch new groups each year. Since 2002, cam-paigns have increased small group participation at our church from 30 percent to 120 percent—seriously! Since 2004 we have had more people in small groups than attend our weekend services. Rather than taking energy from our small groups by forced division, the campaign approach focuses on relationships, not multiplication.

We also do not subscribe to the theory that a small group needs to be kept at an optimum size. Some people are just natural gatherers. They start out with a few people in their small group and then keep inviting others until quite soon they have twenty or thirty people jammed into their house every Tuesday night.

At Saddleback, we don't penalize people who are able to gather others around them. Instead, we encourage groups to become any size they want and then equip them for health in spite of their size. We believe ratios are more important than size, so through subgrouping we help maintain ratios of attendees to leaders at optimum levels so that participation and group health are not jeopardized. In other words, we tell our small group leaders they can grow their group as big as they like and we'll show them how to foster an environment for life-changing, healthy community (this is discussed in detail in chapter 8).

### 9. Empowered Group Members, Not Passive Spectators

One of the questions we are always asked is, where do you find leaders? We have discovered tomorrow's leaders are today's group members. As we begin to share ownership and rotate leadership through the natural flow of group life, we find our best potential leaders in this setting. This is also contrary to traditional group theory that dictates a strong leader teaching listening members. I will unpack this idea in subsequent chapters.

### 10. Master Teacher Curriculum, Not Leaders as Bible Masters

People often are reluctant to become a leader because they have limited biblical knowledge and/or limited time to prepare for group meetings. One of the things we learned through our campaign strategy was that providing an easy-to-use, DVD-based curriculum takes a huge load of responsibility off the shoulders of the small group leaders. Providing a video-based study in which the virtual master teacher leads the group through the study at the beginning of the group session proved to be a win/win for us and the hosts, who merely had to facilitate the discussion after the video. Of course, we provide our leaders with additional tools, but we use master teacher curriculum to start them on the pathway.

## Questions

Which of these points resonated with you?

_____

_____

_____

_____

What areas of small group ministry do you need to rethink?

_____

_____

_____

_____

How is your small group ministry unique? What are the characteristics of your church or ministry that make it different from others?

_____

_____

_____

_____

In one sentence, write down what you are trying to accomplish with your small group ministry.

_____

_____

_____

_____

What are some principles you believe to be true concerning small group ministry?

_____

_____

_____

_____

What are some of the possible benefits?

_____

_____

_____

_____

What is your church's delivery system for developing healthy and balanced disciples?

_____

_____

_____

_____

What is your system for developing leaders in your church?

_____

_____

_____

_____

What is your system for developing small group leaders?

_____

_____

_____

_____

What is your strategy for connecting people into small groups?

_____

_____

_____

_____

What resources and support do you provide for your small group leaders?

_____

_____

_____

_____

What opportunities do the people of your church have for shared leadership?

_____

_____

_____

_____

# 3

# What Did We Learn from the Book of Acts?

## *The Paradigm Shift*

Day after day, in the temple courts and from house to house, they never stopped teaching and proclaiming the good news that Jesus is the Christ.

Acts 5:42

Never doubt that a small group of thoughtful, committed citizens can change the world. Indeed, it is the only thing that ever has.

Margaret Mead

Everything we do in our small group ministry is biblically based. The concept of the five biblical purposes is not something we made up at Saddleback Church. In fact, these biblical purposes go all the way back to the very beginning of the Christian church, as found in the New Testament.

The birth of the church described in the book of Acts was a community of believers without a building; the church did not own a piece of property until centuries later. But in these early days the church experienced explosive growth throughout the city of Jerusalem. In fact, within a matter of a few months, the church included more than 5,000 people. All over the city, both in temple courts (what we would call *church services*) and in house-to-house meetings (*small groups*), they were living out the five biblical purposes of fellowship, discipleship, ministry, evangelism, and worship.

### The First Home Groups

Small groups were foundational to the early church, but what did they do? As we examine this question, we can begin to develop a plan for our own small group ministries. The answer is given to us in Acts 2:42–47:

> They devoted themselves to the apostles' teaching and to the fellowship, to the breaking of bread and prayer. Everyone was filled with awe, and many wonders and miraculous signs were done by the apostles. All the believers were together and had everything in common. Selling their possessions and goods, they gave to anyone as he had need. Every day they continued to meet together in the temple courts. They broke bread in their homes and ate together with glad and sincere hearts, praising God and enjoying the favor of all the people. And the Lord added to their number daily those who were being saved.

The small groups described in Acts that met in homes were a strategic part of the greater church, and the Bible tells us these groups were purpose driven groups. Both the small groups and the greater church (all of the believers) focused on all five of the biblical purposes; they fellowshipped, discipled, ministered, evangelized, and worshiped. And it is particularly significant that they *balanced* the biblical purposes, which is the basis for health. As was true in biblical times, this balance of the purposes is vital to the health of small groups today.

Unfortunately, today most small groups focus on one purpose only. They are a fellowship group, a service group, a discipleship group, or some other kind of group. At Saddleback we found that if we wanted to have a healthy small group ministry, we had to instill the idea of balance into the DNA of the church, into every small group of the church, and into every individual life in the church.

## 1. They Fellowshipped

Membership in the body of Christ means we can identify with a family—God's family. They joined in the fellowship "and ate together with glad and sincere hearts" (Acts 2:46). It has always interested me that right after Jesus was baptized and then tempted in the desert, one of the first things he did was get twelve guys and form a small group. Even Jesus saw the value of relational discipleship in a group context and the need for fellowship.

Are the members of your small groups getting along well? Do they have fun at the meetings? Is there usually lots of laughter and good food? If so, fellowship is happening, right? Not necessarily. Very often fellowship is nothing more than hanging out and having a good time. True fellowship, however, dives below the surface image that people present to the world. True fellowship not only connects members to each other but also connects them to Christ.

## 2. They Were Discipled and Grew Spiritually

The Bible says, "They devoted themselves to the apostles' teaching" (Acts 2:42). That means they devoted themselves to growing in Christ and maturity. Evidently not only did they listen to what the apostles were teaching in the temple courts on the Sabbath and other days, but these people also gathered in their homes and studied and practiced what was being taught in the temple courts.

Doing a Bible study is just one piece of discipleship. Unfortunately, it is often the only piece that most groups accomplish. With intention and focus, however, group members can begin to look at discipleship as not only *learning* about the Word of God but also *living out* its truth in every aspect of their lives through the five biblical purposes. They can begin to identify and take their spiritual next step as well as help others identify theirs.

## 3. They Ministered to Each Other

"They gave to anyone as he had a need" (Acts 2:45). That's ministry: believer to believer. These groups became an outlet for support, ministry, benevolence, charity, and shared meals—all in a group context.

Small groups need to be more than just a meeting that happens every Thursday night; they should be engaged in ministry and meeting the needs of people within the body of Christ. Sometimes the ministry will take place right in your group as people walk through a crisis together. At other times a group member could use his or her unique gifts to help someone in the body.

### 4. They Evangelized the Lost

This was their mission: "And the Lord added to their number daily those who were being saved" (Acts 2:47). If you only go fishing once a week—a weekend service—you are only going to catch fish then. If you go fishing throughout the week—small groups—the number of fish will increase dramatically. When all five biblical purposes are happening within your groups and in the lives of each group member, the natural by-product is evangelism. People are attracted to the kind of changes they see taking place in the lives of healthy Christians.

*Evangelism can happen personally, locally, and globally.*

Every small group has a mission to the world, and while you want your groups to focus on that, you also don't want them to forget the mission field they live in: the people in their neighborhood or circle of influence with whom they interface throughout the week. Small groups are a great place to prompt members to begin praying for their neighbors and friends and even planning activities designed for building bridges with those who are not followers of Christ. Evangelism can happen personally, locally, and globally.

### 5. They Worshiped

"They devoted themselves . . . to the breaking of bread and prayer. . . . [They were] praising God" (Acts 2:42, 47). In other words, these early Christians worshiped in their homes. And what was the result? "Everyone was filled with awe, and many wonders and miraculous signs were done by the apostles" (v. 43). The bottom line is that God shows up when people make room for him.

We need to work at cultivating times of worship in our small groups during which we focus on God's presence and express our love through song, prayer, praise, and other experiences. At the heart of worship is surrender, and small groups can help people live out being a living sacrifice. We are told in the book of Romans: "Therefore, I urge you, brothers, in view of God's mercy, to offer your bodies as living sacrifices, holy and pleasing to God—this is your spiritual act of worship" (12:1). Group life encourages transparency among members as they receive the support they need to succeed in their Christian walk. This increased transparency provides the fertile ground for worship to happen.

## Balance of the Purposes

Each of the five biblical purposes will be addressed in greater detail in subsequent chapters. For right now, however, begin to imagine the potential power that could be released in your church if every small group empowered every individual to live out the biblical purposes in their daily lives as it was in the New Testament. The five purposes should be balanced, but I do not mean balancing all of the purposes during each group meeting (e.g., fifteen to twenty minutes on each purpose each week). Instead, help your groups to self-evaluate on a semiannual basis. Realize that some of the purposes, such as ministry and evangelism, might take a little longer for your groups to embrace, and some of the purposes may need to be accomplished outside the regular group time. The key here is to begin thinking about how to balance the five biblical purposes over periods of six to twelve months. At Saddleback we use tools called the Personal Spiritual Health Plan and Group Health Plan to help groups begin the process and develop a plan to bring health and balance. Again, all of this will be expanded upon in subsequent chapters. For now though, begin to imagine the possibilities.

## Questions

What does the book of Acts reinforce for your current ministry?

_____

_____

_____

How does the book of Acts shape your small group ministry?

_____

_____

_____

Why are you involved in small group leadership?

_____

_____

_____

How do the people of your church get their spiritual needs met?

_____

_____

_____

If your church doubled in size tomorrow, could your people still get their needs met in your present care system? Are your small groups a strategic part of your church?

_____

_____

_____

If so, in what ways do they help your church meet its goals?

_____

_____

_____

If not, how could your small groups be a reflection of your church?

_____

_____

_____

# What Does This Look Like?

4

# Is Your Vision Blurry?

## *Define Success Clearly*

Now, my son, the LORD be with you, and may you have success and build the house of the LORD your God, as he said you would.

1 Chronicles 22:11

In life, as in football, you won't go far unless you know where the goalposts are.

Arnold H. Glasgow

In the years 2000 to 2001, our leadership team began asking the question, What does a healthy follower of Christ look like? As a church, what is our end product? Obviously people are not *products*, but if we are to be successful in fulfilling Christ's commission to us to make disciples, we need to define the term *disciple*. Through a series of meetings, we agreed that a healthy follower of Christ is someone who is balancing the five biblical purposes in his or her life and heart.

A healthy follower of Christ is:

- surrendering his or her heart and life to Christ on an ongoing basis

- experiencing fellowship with other Christians
- growing in Christ through being and action
- discovering and using his or her God-given gifts and abilities
- reaching out and sharing the love of Christ with nonbelievers

Unless you know what the target is, you cannot hit it. For us, the target became health through balance. How do we define that? Take a look at 2 Corinthians 4:18, "But we as Christians have no veil over our faces; we can be mirrors that brightly reflect the glory of the Lord. And as the Spirit of the Lord works within us, we become more and more like him" (TLB). As we begin to reflect Christ and become more like him, the focus of our lives will shift away from self-centeredness and toward serving him through every area of our life. That is health and balance.

*Unless you know what the target is, you cannot hit it.*

## Begin with the End in Mind

So if we as a church were trying to produce healthy followers of Christ, our leadership team had to decide what the best tool or delivery system is to produce that desired result. Eventually we agreed that small groups are the best environment to produce health through balancing the biblical purposes in each person's life.

Why small groups?

1. *They are biblical.* As seen in Acts, from the beginning of the church, Christians have gathered together around the biblical purposes to worship Christ.
2. *They are convenient.* A small group system supplies you with a venue in which it is easy to disseminate information with transformation.
3. *They are economical.* Small groups meeting in homes do not put a strain on your church building or resources. They are self-sustaining.
4. *They are unlimited in size.* As your church grows, just add more groups!
5. *They are unlimited in reach.* Wherever you have people, you can have a small group.

6. *They provide accountability.* Each member has an immediate support system.
7. *They provide a safe environment.* Members can explore their gifts and serving possibilities without feeling vulnerable or exposed.
8. *They provide focus.* If correctly directed, a small group is a collection of people working on common goals—not just one person teaching while the others listen.

Our strategy for making healthy followers of Christ (disciples) is small groups. We have no other plan; we have no other delivery system. We believe this is the most effective way to make disciples and lead people to live healthy and balanced lives. We are not a church *with* small groups; we are a church *of* small groups (see figure 4.1).

**Figure 4.1**
**Church Groups**

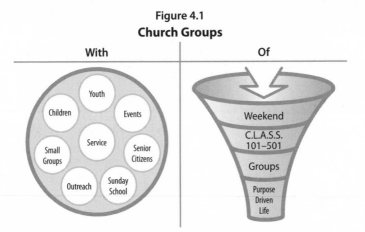

Our small group ministry is not just another program. It is an embedded and integrated piece of everything we do as a church. It's our infrastructure. It's where care happens. It's our delivery system for all spiritual formation. It is our method of balancing the biblical purposes and fostering healthy lives.

## Define Success on All Levels

Every church operates on various levels. Unfortunately, all too often those *levels* are working against each other. We sought to create

alignment—every person and every ministry working to create a healthy
church. It's important that you have harmony through all levels:

> **The Church**—church structure and activities get people into
> groups
>> **Small Group Ministry**—strives to bring health and balance
>> to all groups
>>> **Small Group**—individual groups balance the purposes
>>> for health
>>>> **Individual**—balances the purposes in his or her life
>>>> and heart for health

What is the purpose of your church? Do you have vision and mission
statements? And if so, are they more than well-constructed words? Are
they a reflection of who you are as a church? Do the people of your
church know your vision and mission, and are they in agreement with
it? The best way to get the people of the church in alignment with
its vision and mission is by repeated exposure to them through small
groups. In order to accomplish this, your small group ministry vision
and mission statements must be in alignment with those of the church.
The idea is for everyone to be moving in the same direction—toward
a healthy and balanced life centered on Christ.

Our small group ministry vision and mission statements are both
in alignment with the purpose statement of the church. Everything
we do in small group ministry falls under those two statements.

The purpose statement of Saddleback Church is:

> To bring people to Jesus and membership in his family, develop
> them to Christlike maturity, and equip them for their ministry
> in the church and life mission in the world, in order to magnify
> God's name.

The vision and mission statements of Saddleback's small group ministry are:

> **Vision:** to see every person, from the core of our church to the
> ever-growing community, connected in a healthy small group.
> **Mission:** to help spiritual seekers become transformed believers who
> model Purpose Driven lives and motivate others to do the same.

## Sharing Your Vision

If people gave to every charitable organization based on its need, then every hospital, every food center, every Salvation Army would have more than enough resources. The needs of the world are plentiful. People generally don't give to needs; they give time and resources to a vision. As the leader of the small group ministry, it's important for you to share your vision not only with your team but also with the rest of the congregation, preferably through the lead pastor. Give them the biblical rationale for the things you do within your ministry. Share with them the Scriptures that empower you and give you life. What Scripture guides the vision for your small group ministry? Does everyone know this Scripture and why it was chosen? What do you want to see happen through this ministry?

Strive not to come across as a salesman. The people in your church need to know your heart is in small groups. Share stories from your own small group experiences. Tell them how much your small group means to you. Vision casting for small groups has to make sense to your people, but for it to be the most effective, it is important to touch their hearts. Even better, use testimonies from the people in your church. They are the real satisfied customers!

## Intentionally Shepherding the Sheep

Matthew tells of Jesus going through the towns and villages teaching, preaching, and healing. Imagine him stopping on top of a hill and looking down on the bustling city where crowds of people rush busily through the streets. Matthew 9:36–38 describes his reaction: "When he saw the crowds, he had compassion on them, because they were harassed and helpless, like sheep without a shepherd. Then he said to his disciples, 'The harvest is plentiful but the workers are few. Ask the Lord of the harvest, therefore, to send out workers into his harvest field.'" This passage casts vision that comes straight from the heart of Jesus.

His heart was broken by what he saw, and he was "filled with compassion." The Bible tells us these people were "harassed and helpless," and they had no answers. Perhaps the most telling part of this story is when Jesus very clearly revealed that his heart was not really broken by the troubles or struggles these people were dealing with but rather because they had no shepherd. They had no one to lead them or feed them; they needed someone to guide and provide for them. The heart of the Lord was broken when he saw the poor and leaderless condition of these people.

Today lack of leadership is still an issue and must be a source of pain to the heart of God. The pastor's task is to *make disciples* of the people God has entrusted to his or her leadership and care. But this duty does not merely rest upon the shoulders of the lead pastor or the small group point person or even the small group leader; it rests upon the shoulders of every Christian. This is the vision you must share with your people.

Notice that Jesus's heart broke for an entire city. It is a common mistake for pastors to see their influence as limited to the members of their church. It is also a common mistake for small group leaders and even small group members to see their influence as limited to their small group. Instead, we must learn to see our responsibilities to the people who live within our sphere of influence in our cities, communities, and neighborhoods.

The people Jesus saw were certainly not all believers or members of a church. His heart broke for all of the people—believers or not. We leaders are called upon by God to minister to the world around us regardless of whether they are saved. And it is our responsibility to share that same vision with every member of our church.

*Your small group ministry will not be any stronger than its leaders, and your leaders will not be any stronger than you.*

Have you ever noticed that when you are tuned in to something, you begin seeing it everywhere? You decide to buy a car and you research a certain make and model. Suddenly you see that car everywhere, not because the car is any more popular now than it was before you began your research, but because your eyes are tuned in to that car, so you notice it.

Imagine if the people of your church were tuned in to the "harassed and helpless" (Matt. 9:36), whether that means the Christian sitting next to them in a small group meeting or the nonbeliever who works behind the counter at their favorite coffeehouse. Imagine if they could see people through the eyes of Jesus. How would it change their interactions with each other and with the world at large?

As a leader, it is your job to help them tune in to the harassed and helpless of today, to share Jesus's vision of a shepherd for every person. Your small group ministry will not be any stronger than its leaders, and your leaders will not be any stronger than you. If you aren't modeling a shepherd's heart, your leaders won't buy into the vision. If your heart is not invested in your people, don't expect them to invest their hearts either.

## Sharing the Vision

A great way to share the vision of a shepherd for every sheep is by encouraging your leaders and group members to share experiences with new believers and to spend time with nonbelievers.

### Baptize New Believers

One of my favorite ways to stay focused on people the way Jesus did is by doing or watching baptisms. At Saddleback Church, before we baptize people, we ask them to tell the story of how they found Christ. Listening to the story of how a person was lost and now is found reminds us *why* we do what we do. Let's face it; working in a church would be great if we didn't have to deal with people! But we do. And sitting at the water's edge performing or watching baptisms, or listening to testimony after testimony, recharges my batteries to keep on sharing the vision.

### Hang Out with the Sheep

It is our responsibility to get our hands dirty and hang out with the sheep. A true shepherd smells like the sheep. You can't pick up the smell of the sheep by reading about them; you have to be willing to hang out with them. I love my neighborhood. Do we share the same religious beliefs? No. Do we raise our kids the same? No. Do we party the same? No. But are they people I am glad to call neighbors and friends? In a heartbeat!

I believe in relational evangelism. I want people to *see* Jesus in me before I *tell* them about Jesus. A perfect example is a buddy in my neighborhood. The first time I met him, he made it clear he would never go to church. An interesting statement since I hadn't even talked to him about church—or anything religious! For the next five years, however, we had several spiritual conversations. From his reaction, I was certain I was having no impact on him whatsoever. Then one Monday morning I was running late for work, but in God's timing,

I was right on time. As I came out of the house and hurried to my car, he walked up to me and said, "Hey, do you have a minute?" I was already late, but as he began to talk I could see that he was in a bad place. It was a time of crisis for him and he could have gone to anyone else, but for some reason he waited and came to me on that Monday morning. I decided to be even later for work, and we both headed to Starbucks. We sat for quite some time, him telling me his problems and me listening. And on that Monday morning, that guy who said he would never go to church accepted Christ right in Starbucks without one thought to the other customers sitting around us.

*A true shepherd smells like the sheep.*

Every time I see him, I praise God. For five years I tried to make a difference and didn't see any progress, but in one day, all that changed. My neighbor made a powerful statement that day in Starbucks that I hope gets etched on your heart. He said, "If only I would have done what you have been saying these past five years, I wouldn't be in this mess." Can you imagine how I would have felt if he had said, "I wish you would have told me this five years ago so I wouldn't be in this mess"? I am glad I did my part.

### Beware of Vision Leakage

I like the quote from Richard Nixon—not "I am not a crook,"[1] but when he said, "You know, when I'm tired of hearing it, I know my staff has gotten it. And when my staff is tired of hearing it, I know the press corps has gotten it. And when the press corps is tired of hearing it, I know the nation has gotten it."

So often we make the mistake of failing to cast a vision. Every year our small group team members work around a central theme. Why a theme? It helps the team stay focused on an area I feel the Lord is bringing to my attention. Through prayer, fasting, and seeking the Lord, I use the theme to center the team on a particular area we need to shore up to help accomplish the vision. I give them Scripture and a medallion as a reminder of that theme. In addition, we all go through a book together and use our team meetings to discuss that theme and how we might incorporate it into that year's small group strategy. This might seem like overkill, but I have found we all have short memories. The business of life often derails us, and we lose our focus as we deal with the realities of day-to-day living. To combat that, we leaders must continually keep that vision in front of us, and we must continually keep it in front of our team. (For a list of the themes I have used, visit www.smallgroups.net/themes.)

Your people have to know what the goal is: health and balance. It is not merely getting people into groups, it is transformation. In the book of Nehemiah the Israelites have a vision of rebuilding the wall. It is a fifty-two-day project (Neh. 6:15), but halfway through the project—by day twenty-six—their enemies are trying to get them off course (see Neh. 4). Like the Israelites, we have a tendency to drift away from the core vision (whether from the enemy or circumstances of life), and this tendency can only be remedied by continually emphasizing the vision. The example from Nehemiah is a good illustration; recast and readjust your course for the vision monthly!

### Purpose Brings Focus

Without a clear purpose, your small group ministry will flounder and your small group members will see little value in joining beyond fellowship. Too often small group point people focus more on getting people into small groups than on defining the purpose of the small group ministry. You search for new small group curriculum or creative ways to train your leaders, but the real problem is a lack of focus and purpose. The Bible tells us in Ephesians 5:17, "Therefore do not be foolish, but understand what the Lord's will is." Every church must discover what God's will is for their small group ministry. The small group point person's role is to fulfill that purpose.

I believe my purpose, as a small group point person, is to see the purposes lived out in the life of our groups and in the lives of the individuals in those groups.

### Questions

What does a healthy disciple look like? What are the character traits of a healthy disciple?

_____

_____

_____

_____

What are the vision and mission statements of your church?

_____

_____

_____

_____

What are the vision and mission statements of your small group ministry?

_____

_____

_____

_____

What are the key practices that stimulate spiritual growth?

_____

_____

_____

_____

What is the delivery system for discipleship in your church?

_____

_____

_____

_____

What role do small groups play in the discipleship process?

_____

_____

_____

_____

# 5

## It All Starts with Community

### Build a Foundation for Health and Balance

Finally, all of you, live in harmony with one another; be sympathetic, love as brothers, be compassionate and humble.

1 Peter 3:8

The first service one owes to others in the fellowship consists in listening to them. Just as love of God begins in listening to His Word, so the beginning of love for the brethren is learning to listen to them. It is God's love for us that He not only gives us His Word but lends us His ear. So it is His work that we do for our brother when we learn to listen to Him.

Dietrich Bonhoeffer

Even though fellowship may be the most frequently cited benefit of a small group, it is a mistake to allow groups to stay in the comfort zone of this benefit. True Christian community goes deeper than spending social time together. It dives below the surface into the heart and enables us to speak into each other's lives. It provides the strong foundation for living out all the purposes in a safe environment and is the glue that holds your groups together when times get tough. This type of community will not happen, however, without direction and focused leadership.

Most small groups look like the circle on the left side of figure 5.1, with a primary focus on fellowship. But focused leadership can bring about a healthy balance of the purposes, depicted in the circle on the right side.

**Figure 5.1**

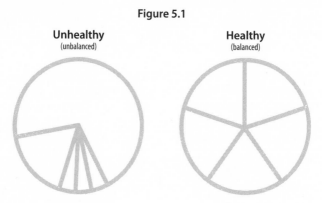

**Unhealthy**
(unbalanced)

**Healthy**
(balanced)

## Direction

Once your group leaders and group members have caught and embraced the vision, it's important to provide direction for their momentum. One of the easiest ways to do this is to provide group guidelines in writing for every group leader. For an example of the small group guidelines that Saddleback uses, see www.smallgroups.net/resources. This lays the foundation for a healthy small group experience and gives the leader an easy way to set expectations and move group members in the same direction.

The small group guidelines tell your small group leaders and members not only *why* they are meeting but also *how* they will set the stage for their meetings. The guidelines might include points on conflict resolution, gossip, and the importance of attendance as well as agreement on day and time of meetings. We recommend our groups go over the guidelines during their first session together. Ideally, the groups should revisit the guidelines once a year or when adding new members.

## Practical Tips

The duty of the small group point person is to help his or her small group leaders by providing direction and suggestions on how they can create and nurture an environment that is conducive to diving below the surface. Following are some practical ways we at Saddleback encourage our small groups to accomplish this.

### Meet in Decentralized Locations

We believe meeting off campus rather than in the church building promotes deeper fellowship within the small group. Home or coffee shop meetings have a more intimate and relaxed atmosphere, which fosters prolonged conversation. Also, members cannot help but feel as though they know each other a little better once they have visited each other's homes. When a home is not available, we have groups that meet in cafes, coffeehouses, restaurants, and workplaces. The idea is to move from meeting in classroom settings in the church to environments that are more conducive to developing community.

In addition, home meetings are simply more practical and good stewardship because your church will not have to add more space to the building for meetings. Your only limitation on space for the small group ministry is the number of houses in which your people live. Even if you have the space in your church to allow groups to meet at your church, I recommend you do not count on that strategy. As your small group ministry grows, it is just a matter of time before you will not have enough rooms, and then you will face the problem of some groups being able to meet at the church while others have to meet at home. It is better to avoid that problem from the beginning.

In subsequent chapters I will discuss how to use meetings on the church campus (centralized) as part of a large group–small group strategy. This can be a strategic method of introducing small groups from a common meeting place (the church) and encouraging people to move into small groups that meet off campus (decentralized).

### Encourage Frequency for Health

We encourage our groups to meet weekly. Although some churches have groups that meet biweekly, the problem with such a schedule is that if a member misses a group meeting, an entire month will pass before he or she will meet with the group again. If your groups meet weekly, a member can miss one meeting and then jump right back in the following week.

### Facilitate Conversation, Don't Just Teach
**Figure 5.2**

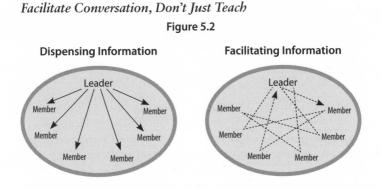

Small group leaders need to move beyond being teachers who dispense information to passive listeners to being facilitators who encourage the exchange of dialogue and discussion among all group members (see figure 5.2). It is important to encourage all members to add to the conversation, which will help them feel their thoughts and comments are valued. This does not only entail simply asking someone, "What do you think about that, Bob?" Instead, leaders should be willing to *throw out the ball* and be quiet as members toss it back and forth to each other instead of merely replying directly to the leader. This moves members from being passive listeners to being engaged participants.

### Let the Bible Be a Normal Part of Their Daily Life

Sometimes groups can get to a point where the only time the Bible is shared is in the *study* part of group life. Encourage group members to make the Bible part of their daily routine, not just something they read for small group study. Encourage your small group leaders to ask simple questions such as, "What verse spoke to you this week?" Just as food is nourishment for our body, the Bible is nourishment for our soul.

Model this behavior in your own life. In email updates, social media, or personal conversations with members of your small group ministry, let them know how the Bible is impacting your life. As you use opportunities to share the Bible, encourage your small group leaders to do the same thing with their group members. The Bible is a living document; let it live through your life and into your small group ministry.

### Shared Ownership

Through our training and verbal vision casting, one of the things we encourage is shared ownership of the group. This begins soon after the group is established through some shared responsibilities. Then it is later expanded when group members become *purpose champions*—group members who are passionate about one of the five biblical purposes and who then encourage other group members to fulfill that purpose. We found when we started talking about those titles up front (fellowship champion, discipleship champion, etc.) that it scared people away; they were hesitant to join a group and take on those responsibilities. This concept will be discussed further in chapter 7, but for now, start thinking about how you can cast vision for shared ownership from the beginning.

*The Bible is a living document; let it live through your life and into your small group ministry.*

When my wife, Lisa, and I first moved to Saddleback, she was in a large, centralized women's group that met at the church. The women met every week as a large group and then divided into assigned groups at tables around the room. Lisa was in charge of fellowship at her table, and when those women do fellowship, it's psychotic. I mean, the money we were spending on food was amazing. Other women at other tables were buying tablecloths and little warmers for casserole dishes and crazy stuff like that. As a guy, I just can't relate. If I am in charge of something like that, I bring a bag of chips and I'm done. You know, that's fellowship to a man. But Lisa was in charge of building the community, and the nine other women at her table were counting on her. The pressure was on.

Now imagine this: It is Tuesday morning and Lisa is in charge of bringing the fellowship to the table and the breaking of the bread. Our newborn daughter, Erika, had been up all night crying. Obviously, Lisa didn't get much sleep. When she finally fell asleep, it was very near morning. All too soon, her alarm goes off. She turns it off with the intention of getting up, but she immediately falls back asleep. When she wakes up later, she realizes she doesn't have as much time to get ready as she would like.

Lisa jumps out of bed, gets dressed, and pulls herself together quickly. Then she turns to me and asks the deadly question: "How do I look?" I have been married long enough to know there is no right answer to that question. If I say, "You look good," then I am a liar. If I say, "You look bad," then I am in even more trouble. So I answer with another question: "How do you think you look?" Okay, we won't go into her response to me.

The point is, would she have even bothered getting out of bed that morning if she did not have a responsibility to the group? No, she would have tried to catch up on a little sleep, reasoning that it wouldn't be a big deal if she didn't show up; she could just catch up the following week. But since she has a responsibility and the group is counting on her to fulfill that duty, she meets with her group that morning.

Without shared ownership of the group, it is easy to slide into poor attendance and eventually just quit coming. Or worse yet, without shared ownership, members may sit in a small group week after week and never develop their giftedness.

### Rotate Leadership

While one person remains the *official* leader of the small group, we encourage our small groups to rotate leadership among members. This accomplishes two things: (1) It develops leadership skills in potential leaders. (2) It forces group members to step out of their comfort zone and gives the entire group the opportunity to support that member in doing so. We realize not everyone will be a great leader, but the key here is moving beyond your comfort zone, and a supportive small group is the perfect place to do so.

*Ask a group member to guide the discussion for a sentence, section, and study.*

Rotating leadership can be done in a few different ways. The leader might start a study by saying, "We are all going to take turns leading during the coming weeks. Who wants to lead next week's study?" Group members then know they are all in the same boat. Everyone is going to lead the discussion at some point.

Another slower method (perhaps best for groups that have been meeting for some time with only one leader) is for the leader to ask a group member to guide the discussion for a *sentence*, *section*, and *study*. Let's say I am leading this small group. One night I turn to Joe and say, "So we have a little more time for discussing this next question. Why don't you take half of the group and go into the dining room for the discussion, and I'll stay in the living room with the other half of the group. It will give us each more time to talk."

Perhaps in a couple more weeks, I will ask Joe to do the same thing with a section of the study. All the while, I am encouraging him and getting feedback from him at the end of the meeting.

In another few weeks an *emergency* comes up. The Lakers are playing tonight, and I really don't want to miss that game. So I call him and say, "Man, Joe, I'm really sick tonight. Would you lead the group through tonight's discussion?" He might say no. But all I have to do at that point is remind him he would be doing the same thing he has already been doing when he led the discussion for a sentence and then a section. He is ready to take the study tonight. So Joe takes the study for the night, and I sit down with a bowl of popcorn to watch the Lakers game.

Okay, that last part would be inappropriate behavior on my part. But the principle is the same whether you are *really* sick or just trying to move someone along the journey: bring members along slowly and empower them to use their leadership skills.

### Attend Services Together

Because our church is large and has multiple services, we encourage groups to meet and attend the same service together. We think it is so important that we make it part of our small group guidelines. This helps build community. The group might share a meal together afterward or just fellowship for a few minutes on the church campus. What happens at the group meeting provides the necessary foundation, but the sure sign of true community is when group members begin spending time together outside of group meetings.

### Grow through Conflict

Group life can have incredible highs and lows. I remember a time when one couple in our group was experiencing the death of a parent. During the same time Lisa and I were buried by issues with our son, Ethan. He is a special needs kid, and at the time we were caught up in learning how to deal with that. As a result, what the couple was going through fell low on our radar. To make matters worse, they were also having a hard time communicating their feelings with the group. What started out as a miscommunication turned into unresolved conflict as time went by. For over a month the four of us struggled with awkwardness whenever we met. We tried to make nice, but it wasn't working.

After realizing the feelings and awkwardness were not going to go away on their own, Lisa and I invited the couple to our house. An hour of small talk went by before I (the tactful one of the group—ha!) said, "Is there an elephant in the room we need to talk about? Is everything okay between us?" After what seemed like a very long pause, each of us started sharing our feelings, which is what Matthew 18:15–17 instructs us to do all along. After a few hours we were in a better place, starting the healing. We brought issues out in the open and prayed together. We learned more about each other and were able to grow through this conflict.

Remember, the enemy doesn't want us to grow closer together and experience true community. So advise your small group leaders to expect the lows, and train them how to use conflict to mature through the tough times.

### Minister to One Another

When we care about one another and we know one another's needs, it's easier to put love into action. We don't hesitate to help.

A few years ago I was the recipient of *love into action*. I was in the middle of a staff meeting when my cell phone rang. I saw that it was my wife, Lisa, so I answered quickly and quietly. The "quietly" part didn't last long. You know how you can often hear conversations on other people's cell phones when you are sitting near them? Well, soon those around me in the room heard my wife on the other end of the phone.

I had two options. I could continue to listen (along with everyone else) or hang up and quickly shut my phone off. That, of course, would entail telling my wife that I had mysteriously lost my signal. I fought my dark side and continued to listen and excused myself out of the room.

She wasn't having a good day. I could hear the kids adding to the mayhem in the background as she tried to tell me how our clothes dryer had just broken. It wasn't just the dryer breaking but a series of events that she had experienced throughout the day. At that point she just wanted to share the issues of the day with me. As I listened, I gave some more thought to the option of hanging up, but that would have brought male stupidity to a whole new level! I listened to her until she could fully explain the situation and we ended the conversation.

After I hung up, one of the guys in my small group (who happened to also be on staff and overheard the conversation) had something helpful to say. "I'll take care of that," he said simply.

"No, no," I told him. "You have enough work to do. This is my problem."

"I can do it because I have a spare dryer in my garage," he insisted. He then left the office, drove to his house, picked up the dryer, and drove to my house to install it. Then he realized he didn't have the right connection for the dryer, so he made a trip to the hardware store to pick up another one. After doing so, he successfully installed the new dryer and then even got rid of our old dryer.

I have to admit, it was tough on me to be on the *receiving* end of service. But I can also tell you that I appreciated him going the extra mile, and it definitely deepened our connection. The next day I called him to let him know my refrigerator was on the blink! Not really. I called to say thanks!

It is also easier to define and use one another's gifts in community. Very often it takes someone else to point out and validate our spiritual gifts. A small group is the perfect environment for identifying a person's gifts and suggesting next steps. The consistency of meetings also provides built-in accountability *if* true community exists and members feel comfortable following up with each other.

### Be Lovingly Passionate in Evangelism

When we know a small group member is hurting over loved ones who don't know Christ yet, we are more motivated to pray for them to be saved. It is also easier to invite nonbelievers into a group atmosphere for a social gathering than to invite them to a small group or church. People who are resistant to church just might agree to drop by for a barbecue. And if those people see true community reflected in your small group, that atmosphere is quite hard to resist.

Bill started attending a men's small group during a Life's Healing Choices study. He attended Saddleback Church occasionally with his wife, and she was the one who encouraged him to give the small group a try. He was a bit older than the rest of the guys, and he walked with a limp. He was hesitant to share much about his life, but eventually he told the group he was a former Marine pilot. As an officer, he had been in charge of many men and was accustomed to the role of leader. That all changed the night he had a stroke and was hospitalized for a little more than three months. No longer a strong-willed, sharp jet pilot, he felt he had been reduced to a feeble, slow-talking, hard-of-hearing, crippled man. Lost in despair and depression, at one point he quit attending group and only came back after his wife *made him*.

The group became even more committed to helping Bill see God's plan for his life. Many of the guys in the group who had struggled with their own sense of identity began speaking into his life and directing him toward Scripture. At one point, he surrendered and asked God to help him let go of the past and learn to live in the present. It was a turning point in his life as he decided to make Christ his Commanding Officer.

Not long after that he heard that one of his co-workers was in the hospital after suffering a brain aneurysm. After finding out that none of his co-workers had visited the man, Bill began to visit him every week. The man could not talk or even acknowledge that someone was in the room. After Bill shared this with his small group, they encouraged him to pray for the man instead of just sitting silently week after week. Bill did just that. Eventually the man was on the road to recovery, acknowledging visitors, looking forward to Bill's visits, eating on his own, and slowly making progress.

Now Bill never misses a small group meeting. In fact, he always shows up twenty minutes early, and this tough Marine is always one of the first to offer hugs of encouragement to the other men in the small group.

### Go on Mission Trips Together

Few things push small groups beyond their comfort zone more than a mission trip. Read the experience of a member in one of our small groups:

> My wife and I were so excited on that Sunday night in 2003 when Pastor Rick and his wife, Kay, outlined a new missions strategy they called P.E.A.C.E. It was so clear to both of us that God wanted us to do this. By the end of the message God had spoken to our hearts so strongly that we simply had no choice. We brought the idea up to our small group at the next meeting and, just as clearly, no one else had felt the call we'd experienced. We invited one of the couples to dinner

and asked them again if they would be willing to accompany us on a trip. After a few days of praying about our request, they agreed.

Our objective was to reach an unreached people group in West Africa. The people were Muslim, the area was contested by Christians and Muslims, and the environment was severe: high heat, humidity, bugs, and disease. Despite the obstacles, we knew we were called to go, so we made the contacts, did the preparation, and flew off on a two-week trip.

In many villages 70 percent of the children were dying before the age of five, mainly due to waterborne disease. What little health care existed was sparse, often just a tiny little clinic with a few analgesics located miles from most villages. Ill people were often forced to trek up to fifteen miles on foot to a clinic. Most died along the way or soon after they arrived, victims of a toxic mix of malnutrition and disease. Children had little prospect of education. While elementary education was free, the cost of the pencils, paper, and books was simply too great for most subsistence farmers to bear. So there was no way to break the crushing cycle of poverty that trapped them.

Two weeks later while sitting in our hotel in Europe as we prepared for the return trip to California, my wife and I were haunted by the faces of the children and adults who had stared at us looking for hope. We knew we had to go back.

When we returned home and reported to our small group, we immediately announced that we would be returning in five months and asked other members to pray about going with us. The couple who had gone the first time couldn't take time off to return to Africa so quickly, but four other people in the small group stepped up.

Five months later, six of us were on a plane heading to West Africa for eighteen days. One husband and wife are both physicians, and they left their preschool-age children in their inner-city apartment with a grandmother who spoke only Portuguese.

Our destination was a country that is a petri dish for the worst diseases on the planet, where bandits own the roads after dark, where people die of exotic and mysterious maladies, where Islam and Christianity meet in violent and dramatic forms, and where people are dying without Christ. The trip was traumatic and filled with spiritual warfare to an extent we had never experienced, but despite many challenges that required God's hand of safety and protection, we returned safely home with amazing stories and many praises to report.

A week or two later our small group was being interviewed on video at Saddleback. The couple who are both doctors were late. My cell phone rang, and as I answered I heard the sounds of crying and sirens over the phone. The husband was shouting that they had been in a terrible accident. They had been turning into the church parking lot on a green turn signal when an oncoming driver of a very large SUV blew through a red light and broadsided their aging Toyota Corolla. I ran to the intersection only to learn that the family was being transported to the hospital and no one knew their condition. As I looked at their demolished compact car, it seemed obvious that no one could have escaped the collision alive.

Driving to the hospital, I was filled with all kinds of fearful thoughts, all of which vanished when we learned the miraculous news in the emergency room. The wife had suffered a broken collarbone—her car door was the point of impact. The little boy in the seat behind her had a small piece of safety glass stuck in his scalp, but it was removed without stitches. The husband and other son were unscathed. All were released that night.

Because they trusted in God for the outcome, this family had dismissed the three great concerns about global missions—job, children, and personal safety. As a result, they were totally protected during the mission trip. But you can't miss the tongue-in-cheek irony: it's more dangerous to turn into a church parking lot than it is to go on a global mission trip!

After the second trip, we waited one year and then returned to West Africa with six more members of our small group. In three trips over seventeen months, fourteen people from our small group went to this area. By our last trip, five churches in the area were actively engaged in reaching this people group, and one church not only had established a church in the heart of the people but also claimed a dozen new believers. The fourteen people from our small group who traveled with us ranged in age from twenty-one to seventy-nine and were business and career people, housewives, singles, and retired people. None claimed any expertise in missions or even evangelism. All testified that they witnessed the hand of God doing miracles in their midst. For some, it was the pinnacle moment of their life.

God does not require that we be able, only that we are willing. He is able.

### Encourage Members to Meet Socially

An important part of building a healthy small group is extending the sense of community into social settings, which gives group members a chance to see another side of each other. Obviously I don't act the same in my small group as I act at a baseball game. (It would scare people away if I did.) When group members get to know each other outside the boundaries of group meetings, a whole new dimension is added to their relationships. It's like looking at a house from two different directions: Viewing it from the north, you describe the house as having four windows and a red door. Viewing it from the south, you describe the house as having two doors and three windows. Both statements are true, but they are from different perspectives. The same can be said of people in small groups. Knowing them only in the context of a small group meeting is like viewing a house from the north side; your view is limited. Seeing people from various perspectives will give you insights into their life.

### Share Family History

When group members experience genuine community and unconditional love, they become more willing to be honest and vulnerable with one another. When we are part of a true community, we feel safer to talk more openly and share parts of our history that may be painful.

I experienced this in my own small group during a trip we took together. One of our stops was Manzanar Internment Camp. Located at the foot of the Sierra Nevada, about 230 miles northeast of Los Angeles, this camp had housed Japanese Americans after the bombing of Pearl Harbor.

Two of our small group members were of Japanese descent, but I didn't know that the mother of one of them had been imprisoned at this very camp. As we looked around we came to a wall that listed all the names of the people who had been brought to the camp. Halfway down a column was the name Sachiko Nakashima. Tyra told me that was his mother.

*When group members experience genuine community and unconditional love, they become more willing to be honest and vulnerable with one another.*

A whole new level of closeness developed between Tyra and me as we embraced and cried. He was crying for his mother, who had been stripped of all her earthly possessions and held in this place for years. I was crying for my friend's pain as he remembered what she had been through.

When we planned that trip, I had no way of knowing what the result would be. It was just another interesting historical site until I witnessed my friend's reaction. It took the two of us, and our entire small group, to a deeper level of community and surrender. Perhaps it was not your typical worship experience, but I am reminded of

Romans 12:15 that says blessed are those who "weep with those who weep" (NLT). This type of sharing would not have been possible without first establishing true and honest community.

### Vacation Together

Ephesians 2:19 is a key verse about fellowship. "So you are no longer strangers and outsiders. You are citizens together with God's people. You are members of God's family" (NIrV). Godly fellowship enables us to experience true family. We encourage our groups to have parties, eat meals together, go to sporting events, and even take vacations together.

One vacation that my small group took together was particularly memorable. At the time, most of us had small children and even smaller budgets, but we decided to all go on a vacation together despite those facts. We knew someone who had a house in the mountains, so we all stayed there. Sounds great, huh? A grand lodge nestled against the backdrop of the mountains. But the reality was a little different. It was a very small condo with one bedroom and a loft! We put the ladies in the bedroom, the guys in the loft, and the kids lined up sleeping bag against sleeping bag on the living room floor.

Each family took turns preparing a meal. We did morning activities and afternoon activities, and the kids all put on a skit after dinner. (I actually had my first starring role as Stevezilla in one of their skits.) After the kids settled down at night, the adults gathered together and had the equivalent of a small group meeting in the one bedroom.

There were six adults and eight kids cramped in that small condo. My family has gone on other vacations together that were a bit more luxurious (they would have to be), but do you know the vacation we all remember the most? The crazy one where we stayed with our small group in the one-bedroom condo in the mountains!

### Follow Each Other on Social Media

Groups that use social media tools such as Facebook and Twitter create an ongoing conversation with each other. Members know more of what is going on in each other's daily lives through constant updates or *tweets*. Such a connection allows group members to build deeper relationships and spend more group time going deeper because there is less to catch up on. You can also use email, texting, IM, Facebook chatting, pictures, and other technology to enhance group life.

## Questions

How do you define true Christian community?

_____

_____

_____

What intentional strategy does your church use to build community among your members?

_____

_____

_____

What small group vision are you sharing with your volunteers, leaders, and staff?

_____

_____

_____

In what ways do you model your vision?

_____

_____

_____

What type of training is in place to teach small group leaders to delegate group responsibility? Do you have a set of small group guidelines?

_____

_____

_____

If not, what kind of values do you want your small group members to agree upon?

_____

_____

_____

What kind of items (childcare, location of meetings, snacks, etc.) do you want your small group members to agree upon?

_____

_____

_____

Which of the suggestions discussed would you like to see happen more consistently in your small group ministry?

_____

_____

_____

# 6

# Leading for Spiritual Formation

## *How to Create a Church of Disciples, Not Attendees*

And the Lord—who is the Spirit—makes us more and more like him as we are changed into his glorious image.

2 Corinthians 3:18 NLT

The survey suggests that nearly 120 million adults are seeking to become more spiritually adept. To accomplish that goal, they need guidance, a plan of action and some realistic forms of accountability. Doing more of the same activity that got them where they are today is not the solution to getting them to where they want to be tomorrow.

September 2004 survey by the Barna Group

In the average church, what do we do for a person who comes to Christ? If we do anything at all, we send them to a new believer class. I'm not sure that's the best step. We have had new believer classes at Saddleback, and we want to keep orienting people to the basic truths of the Christian life as they get started in their walk, but I think something else is even more important for accomplishing that. Think about this in the physical realm. If new believers are spiritual babies, what do babies need most? Do they need education first? No. They need love, attention, care, nurturance, and protection. New Christians need those same things. Can they get those things in a new believer class? Probably not. They get those things from relationships with other Christians. Where is the best place to develop strong relationships with other Christians? In a small group.

## Discipleship Is Relational

Our number one strategy for helping new believers is to get them into a small group. Once they are part of a spiritual family, we know they will get the guidance they need for their spiritual walk. Like infants, early in their journey the thing new Christians need most is a family. On the other hand, adding a new believer to a small group can enrich the spiritual journey of group members who are more mature in their faith. Any time you encourage another in his or her faith, you also build your own. God does not want us to merely rest in our spiritual maturity; he wants us to use that maturity to guide and coach others.

### Help Groups Understand Their Role

This type of guiding and coaching will not happen in your groups unless your small group leaders know they are your disciple makers. Now, we don't tell our leaders this during the first week, or even during the first month. But as time progresses, they are exposed to increased levels of training until they are fully aware of our expectations of them. The leaders need to understand that their small groups are the best place for discipleship and that members of their group are showing up not just for a Bible study, but to learn truths they can take home and apply to real-life situations as a part of spiritual health. As members wrestle with these truths and incorporate them into their lives, small group meetings take on a greater value for both members and leaders. Furthermore, once members have the opportunity to actually see and become part of the discipleship process, they begin not only to encourage spiritual growth in each other but also to fully expect it to be a by-product of group life.

### The Goal Is Transformation, Not Information

Historically, American churches have operated on the belief that discipleship is about gaining knowledge. If we can fill believers' minds with facts from the Bible and if they memorize enough Scripture, then we have made disciples. Today, churches are questioning this line of thinking. Biblical knowledge is important, but most American Christians know far more than they are putting into practice.

Discipleship is not merely teaching; teaching is often too passive. We need to involve ourselves in the lives of other people. This seldom happens in a classroom setting, but it can happen within a small group if the members have that expectation. One of the protests people make when asked to be a small group leader is, "I don't know enough about the Bible to teach a small group." Our reply is, "Great. We don't want just Bible teachers." In fact, teachers often make ineffective small group leaders because they are too accustomed to doing all of the talking. We want a group of people who are all involved in the discipleship process, not a teacher and a roomful of students.

*When your people are presented with an opportunity to grow, a certain degree of risk is always involved.*

Similarly, your job as a small group point person is not just to care or teach but to develop each person within your sphere of care to balance the Great Commission and the great commandment for spiritual health. You do that by providing low-risk opportunities for growth.

## Opportunity and Risk, Fear and Faith

When your people are presented with an opportunity to grow, a certain degree of risk is always involved (see figure 6.1). It may be a risk of time or money or a risk of stepping out of a comfort zone. At that

**Figure 6.1**

moment, they have two options: step out in faith or be paralyzed by fear and refuse to move at all. The key to preventing paralysis is lowering the bar of risk and providing your people with opportunities to become involved at a *crawl* level. Once they have been successful at the crawl level, which builds their faith, then you can ask for a *walk* commitment. Unfortunately, very often churches place the entry bar too high and ask immediately for a *run*. Doing so almost ensures your people will be paralyzed by fear and refuse your request. The risk level is just too high. If you lower the bar and ask for a crawl commitment, you have reduced the risk and increased the likelihood of getting a positive response.

In 1 Samuel 17 we see a wonderful example of the opportunity-risk or fear-faith cycle played out in the life of David. His first opportunity was shepherding sheep. David was quite young, so perhaps he was a little fearful of such responsibility. He accepted the risk, however, and it built his faith. His next opportunity came in the form of a bear. He took the risk and killed the bear, and his faith continued to grow. David must have realized that whenever he stepped out of his comfort zone in faith, God guided and protected him. The risk level continued to increase, and next David was faced with a lion. He took the risk and killed the lion, and his faith grew. Then one day he came face-to-face with Goliath, the mighty giant. You already know how that story ends, but tell me, how do you think it might have ended if Goliath was David's *first* opportunity for risk? Would he have stepped forward in faith, or would he have turned and run for the hills? He was able to face the seemingly impossible task of slaying Goliath with a handful of rocks because he had already walked through what we at Saddleback call the crawl, walk, run stages.

Everybody has a threshold of pain or risk they are willing to accept. Their response to a new challenge or opportunity is going to be determined by the degree of risk and their degree of faith. If your people's degree of faith does not match the degree of risk, they are going to avoid the opportunity for growth. On the other hand, if you lower the risk, you will provide opportunities for their faith to grow. Then at the next opportunity, not only will they be more likely to take a risk, but they will be able to move up to a new level of risk.

One of the things we discovered was that asking people to become small group *leaders* was just too big a risk. Before that we had asked for lay pastors—an even bigger risk. Eventually, instead of asking for small group leaders or lay pastors, we asked for H.O.S.T.s. A H.O.S.T. is someone who has a *Heart* for people and is willing to *Open* their place to their group, *Serve* a snack, and *Turn* on the DVD. When we asked people if they could host a group in their home, they were very willing. If we had asked those same people to *lead* a small group, most likely they would have said no, even though the responsibilities are the same. I will go into the H.O.S.T. strategy in more detail in chapters 12 and 13.

> *Because David was faithful in stepping out over and over again, ultimately God gave him the opportunity for which he was born.*

Because David was faithful in stepping out over and over again, ultimately God gave him the opportunity for which he was born. It is found in Psalm 78:72, which is the benchmark of our small group ministry: "He cared for them with a true heart and led them with skillful hands" (NLT). God moved David from shepherding sheep to shepherding the nation of Israel based on two qualifications: a true heart and a skill. He developed those qualities by taking David through the crawl, walk, run phases. As David's faith was built, his skill was also built, and he was able to take increasing risks. This is a foolproof system if you develop it intentionally and provide opportunities at every level.

## Next Steps

A small group provides the perfect venue not only for encouraging individual members to take next steps of faith but also for encouraging the entire small group to take these steps together. In order for that to happen, it is important to *balance* the health of the individual and the health of the group and suggest specific next steps for both.

### Individual Growth

- Encourage every member to take the Spiritual Health Assessment on an annual basis (see chapter 10). This tool provides specific opportunities for spiritual growth at every level.
- Encourage every member to create a Spiritual Health Plan on an annual basis (also in chapter 10). Until your group members

create their own *next steps* and put their plans into writing, they are not likely to take action.

- Encourage every member to pair up with another same-sex member of the group for accountability. Once your members have their plan in writing, they need to share that plan with someone who can encourage and support them.
- Encourage every member to always be looking for their spiritual next step. Small group leaders don't need to know all of their members' next steps, but they do need to know who is keeping them accountable.

As an example, I don't expect the members in my own couples' small group to be able to coach me on all the issues of my life because I am in full-time ministry and we have a special needs kid. They simply don't have the life experience to advise me in either area. But I do expect them to know what I am working on spiritually and who is keeping me accountable. Each year when Lisa and I develop our Spiritual Health Plan, I copy it and give it to the guys in that group. These are people I see weekly, and they need to be able to ask me where I am spiritually. If they don't know what I am working on, that is much more difficult.

### Group Growth

- Encourage your groups to use the Spiritual Health Assessment to see the areas where their members need to grow spiritually as a starting point for curriculum and for their Group Health Plan (see chapter 10). For example, if most people in a group score low on evangelism, that group might want to do an evangelism study next.
- Encourage the group to design a Group Health Plan (see chapter 10) to determine what they need to do to grow in balance and health as a small group. For example, if your group wants to grow in the area of worship, they could plan an expression of worship at a group meeting.

## Start Small

I am in two small groups: a couples' group with my wife and a men's group with nine other men. I am not recommending that all ministry leaders should be in two groups, but it works for me. Lisa and I enjoy being in a small group together, but meeting with a group of men adds another dimension to my spiritual walk, and I like hanging out with these guys.

Not too long ago one of the guys in this group had some extra time on his hands because his employer was doing some restructuring. Although Matt was still employed, he wasn't working as much, which meant he and I had more time to meet for coffee. One day we were talking about what he could do with all of that extra time, and I challenged him to try some spiritual exercises. He agreed, and we started by reading some books together and then moved on to do the Spiritual Health Assessment together.

Matt is a solid believer, has his spiritual act together, has a healthy marriage, and is a leader of leaders. Although he had no major issues, I still wanted to challenge him to take a spiritual next step, so I asked him if he would do a forty-day fast with me. Once the shock of that wore off, I asked him to do a five-day fast, which suddenly seemed a lot more reasonable. Matt is in shape, but he likes his food. So although he was game, it was definitely a new spiritual journey for him.

During the fast we met each day at Starbucks to drink water and share spiritual insights. Each day I shared something, but his answer was always the same: "I got nothing but hunger pains!" I told him the idea was not necessarily to come up with *something*; instead, fasting is a spiritual discipline, and God is pleased. At the time, I don't think he was entirely convinced.

At sundown on the fifth day, we broke the fast. Matt had travel plans the following day and called me quickly from the airport when he landed at his destination and said, "I don't have time to talk, but on my flight God opened up the floodgates, and I have a vision for a new company. I can't wait to tell you about it."

After they heard about the spiritual impact of Matt's experience, the rest of our men's group wanted to try fasting, and we all did a four-day fast together. Matt is a leader, and his leadership influenced the other eight guys in the group. Before Matt's experience, if I had asked the entire group to do a fast with me, would they have agreed? Probably not. But after hearing about Matt's experience, they were convinced of the value of fasting.

Teach your group leaders to start small—perhaps challenging only one or two people to join them in a spiritual exercise. Although it might work to ask the entire group to do this, I have seen it work best when you start small. Then as the group members witness a transformation in another person's life, they may ask to be part of it. Ideas for some other spiritual disciplines you can inject into group life can be found at www.smallgroups.net/spiritualgrowth.

## Balanced Curriculum Plan

Use small group curriculum that is biblically based, rather than just self-help material, in order to help group members grow in the five biblical areas outlined in the group plan. This requires a balanced plan of study to guide your small group toward health: each year study one book of the Bible, one spiritual-growth study, and one life-stage study.

*Teach your group leaders to start small— perhaps challenging only one or two people to join them in a spiritual exercise.*

Part of a small group point person's job is reviewing and recommending small group studies. Once you have compiled a list, make it available for your small group leaders to easily access—either online or as a simple printed list they can pick up after the weekly service. Put studies in the order you think will work best. See www.smallgroups.net/resources for examples.

## Keep It Interesting

Jesus certainly wasn't boring, and your small group discipleship elements shouldn't induce sleep either. Regularly check with your groups to find out which studies are enjoyable and which promote spiritual growth. Also ask for specifics about the studies they are not enjoying. We use a simple Small Group Evaluation to track what is working for our groups and what is not. See www.smallgroups.net/free for examples.

The best discipleship plan is relational, incremental (crawl, walk, run), and holistic. Christ challenged his disciples in the same way. He built a relationship with them by initially asking them to merely follow him. Then as they developed, he challenged them to grow in every aspect of their being—not just in head knowledge.

## Questions

What are the key practices that stimulate spiritual growth in your group?

_____

_____

_____

_____

What role do groups play in the discipleship process?

_____

_____

_____

_____

What do you do to encourage groups to balance their curriculum choices?

_____

_____

_____

_____

What type of crawl, walk, run opportunities do you have for the people of your church?

_____

_____

_____

_____

What type of crawl, walk, run opportunities do you have for your small groups?

_____

_____

_____

_____

We have found curriculum to be very powerful and strategic in help-ing groups grow in their weak areas. How do you use curriculum as part of your discipleship process?

_____

_____

_____

_____

What resources for spiritual development do you provide for your leaders?

_____

_____

_____

_____

7

# Don't Lead Alone

*Mobilize Your Groups from Sitting to Serving*

God has given each of you a gift from his great variety of spiritual gifts. Use them well to serve one another.

1 Peter 4:10 NLT

[Rick] Warren didn't invent the cellular church. But he's brought it to an amazing level of effectiveness. The real job of running Saddleback is the recruitment and training and retention of the thousands of volunteer leaders for all the small groups it has.

Robert Putnam, Harvard political scientist and author
of *Bowling Alone*

People often fail to serve, not because they don't want to serve, but because they feel they have nothing to offer or they have not been offered specific opportunities. Churches all across North America are full of overworked pastors and underused members. That is not God's plan; it is a problem, and one that is seen as far back as the Old Testament.

Exodus 18:13–26 tells the story of Moses being overworked and the advice given to him by his father-in-law, Jethro, that solved the problem.

*The Problem*: Moses carried a very heavy workload and was burning out. Each day he took his seat as judge, and anybody with a complaint came to him expecting him to solve their problems. The process took all day, starting in the morning and continuing through the evening. Upon seeing the long hours his son-in-law was working, Jethro told Moses, "What you are doing is not good. You and these people who come to you will only wear yourselves out. The work is too heavy for you; you cannot handle it alone" (Exod. 18:17–18).

*The Solution*: Jethro told Moses to divide the ministry among other God-fearing, trustworthy leaders. He said to Moses, "You've got to be the people's representative before God. You've been spending all your time talking to the people on behalf of God. You've got all that backward, Moses. You need to spend more of your time talking to God on behalf of the people. You've got to spend more time in prayer." Then he told Moses that he had to teach the Israelites how to live. They needed to be taught the precepts and principles of the Torah that would guide their lives so he wouldn't have to deal with so many issues and problems among them.

*The Strategy*: Moses set up a tiered structure of leadership. He appointed leaders of thousands, leaders of hundreds, leaders of fifties, and leaders of tens. Jethro advised him, "Have them serve as judges for the people at all times, but have them bring every difficult case to you; the simple cases they can decide themselves. That will make your load lighter, because they will share it with you" (Exod. 18:22). Our churches are full of people who are willing and capable to share the workload. We only need to ask and encourage them.

*The Result*: Moses was relieved, others were given the opportunity to serve God, and everyone had their needs satisfied. Verse 23 tells us, "If you do this and God so commands, you will be able to stand the strain, and all these people will go home satisfied."

Part of my personal journey mirrors Moses's bad example. I tried to be everything to everybody and meet every need. After all, that's what a pastor is supposed to do—right? Wrong! God never intended for the church to be run by hired guns who do all of the work while the members show up for the weekend show. If you are a ministry leader who is not sharing the workload with the people of your church, not only are you jeopardizing your own health and stamina, but you are robbing your people of an opportunity to serve God.

As a church leader, your job is *not* to do everything. No matter what your level of involvement in ministry, whether you are the lead pastor, an elder, a small group point person, or a small group leader, your job is not only to use your giftedness but also to help others use theirs. And you can do that by doing four things:

1. *Know.* Help them understand the biblical concept of serving through consistent teaching.
2. *Grow.* Help them grow by developing their *sweet spot* in ministry.
3. *Go.* Help them serve by providing them specific and multiple opportunities for service.
4. *Show.* Help them feel appreciated by showing your gratitude throughout the year.

We will spend the rest of this chapter looking at how you might do those four things.

### Know: Help Them Understand the Biblical Concept of Serving through Consistent Teaching

Before you can help your members find their place in ministry, they have to understand serving isn't just another way of getting them more involved in a church program. The concept of ministry comes straight from God's Word. Teach them they are part of the body; they have been gifted by God and their gifts are meant to be used to serve and glorify him. First Corinthians 12:12–27 tells us the body of the church is just like the individual body—made up of many parts, each with a specific purpose.

Give people opportunities to understand this biblically. But more importantly, make sure not only that you understand the biblical concept of serving but that you, as a leader, also buy into it. Do you really believe every person in your church has a special contribution to make, and are you always looking for a way to get everyone involved?

As leaders, how can we accomplish this? Here are some suggestions:

### Every Member Is a Minister

As church leaders, we need to *give the ministry away* to the members of the church. As the congregation becomes more involved in ministry, the pastors are able to spend more time praying, teaching, and equipping. Churches like to *say* every member is a minister, but do we really *believe and act upon* it? Dietrich Bonhoeffer writes,

> In a Christian community, everything depends on whether each individual is an indispensable link in a chain. The chain is unbreakable only when even the smallest link holds tightly with the others. A community which allows to exist within itself members who do nothing, will be destroyed by them. Thus it is a good idea that all members receive a definite task to perform for the community, so that they may know in times of doubt that they too are not useless and incapable of doing anything. Every Christian Community must know that not only do the weak need the strong, but also that the strong cannot exist without the weak. The elimination of the weak is the death of the community.[1]

What do we really believe about the people sitting in our church and in our small groups? Do we believe:

they have the Holy Spirit leading them?

they have been given gifts by God?

they are to use those gifts for the edification of the body of Christ?

If all of that is true, then it is our duty to turn them loose and let them serve so they can meet each other's needs.

When problems arise in the lives of people in our small groups at Saddleback, we don't want them to call the church. We want them to talk with their small group leader and respond to the need together. When it comes to hospital visitation or meeting an immediate need, members of their small groups are the first ones to show up. Read the story of Kevin and Susan:

> In late 2001 we had just gotten our youngest daughter off to college and were planning to move into the empty nester stage. It turned out

God had different plans. We found out we were going to start all over—Susan was pregnant. Once we got over the shock, we started planning on raising one more child.

At the thirty-ninth week we had our last doctor's visit. All was well, and we scheduled a C-section. That weekend Susan noticed the baby wasn't as active as before, but she figured it was not unusual. On Monday she called our doctor to let him know about this, and he had her come in. He was struggling to find the heartbeat and sent her to the hospital for some further tests.

*As church leaders, we need to give the ministry away to the members of the church.*

As I drove to the hospital, I called one of our small group members and asked that the small group keep us in prayer. The test at the hospital revealed the same—they couldn't find a heartbeat. It turned out Chloe's umbilical cord had gotten wrapped around her waist and leg. It was determined that we had probably lost her that Friday.

Susan and I were devastated beyond words. One by one members of our small group started arriving at the hospital. In the middle of the day, they all dropped what they were doing, left work, left the gym, left whatever they were doing, and came to be with us. They spent that afternoon and evening with us, praying with us, crying with us, hugging us. The following morning our doctor induced labor. And once again our small group was there to support us. One member who is a teacher hired a substitute so she could be there with us. Even though they were a room away, we knew they were there for us.

The doctor delivered Chloe, the nurses put her in a dress we'd brought, and then they left us to spend some time alone with her. Words can never adequately describe what it's like for a dad to hold his dead daughter in his arms. We can't even imagine how much tougher this would have been if we had to go through it without our small group. Being part of a small group, having them go through this with us, having them share our joy in the beginnings and share our hurt in the end was such a blessing.

We went through a brutally tragic situation, but having our small group with us took some of the brutality out of it. With God and our small group, we traveled through this journey. And fourteen months later they were there with us again when our daughter Sophie was born. We are grateful for Sophie, comforted that Chloe is with God, and blessed to have our small group family.

The people in our small groups at Saddleback do not hesitate to jump in and provide this type of support because we *continually* tell them, "You are the ministers." We tell *every one* of our members, "You are a minister of Jesus Christ." But more importantly, we *believe* that.

### Model Servanthood

It's not what's taught—it's what's caught. People in your church are waiting to see if you are going to share the ministry. It is not enough to *tell* people; you have to model the behavior in your own ministry. You have to *ask* for their involvement and then make it easy for them to be involved. It is so empowering to work at a church where our senior pastor doesn't just say, "Every member is a minister"; he models it. Rick Warren has almost 400 volunteers assisting in his area of ministry alone.

*It's not what's taught—it's what's caught.*

The only way you are going to create opportunities for biblical servanthood is to let go of your ministry, and leaders of the church should be the first to model that. Take an inventory of your job and ask: What do I love? What do I like? What am I doing that someone else could do? Sometimes the best thing to happen in your church is for it not to happen. Every time you do something not in your gifting, the Holy Spirit can't convict someone else to step in and help through their giftedness.

## Grow: Help Them Grow by Developing Their *Sweet Spot* in Ministry

My dad was a baseball player. He played in high school as a catcher, and he was the first guy to get a full ride baseball scholarship at his college. Then he was invited by the Washington Senators (now the Minnesota Twins) to come and try out (the baseball draft started years later, in 1963). He tried out and was told to do some more conditioning and put some weight on. He never had the chance to go back, however, because World War II started and he entered the military.

Dad never got to play professionally, but he was able to use his baseball expertise to coach me. He was a great coach for me, but unfortunately, I wasn't a great player for him (I was more gifted for football). One thing I will always remember, however, is that when he coached me on batting, he used to tell me to hit with the *sweet spot* of the bat. This is the part of the bat that gives you the most powerful hit and the least vibration to your hands when it connects with the ball. You can hit with any part of the bat, but it is the most powerful when you find the *sweet spot*. That's what we want for each person's spiritual life. "What engineers give sports equipment, God gave you. A zone, a region, a life precinct in which you were made to dwell. He tailored the curves of your life to fit an empty space in his jigsaw puzzle. And life makes sweet sense when you find your spot."[2] You can do many things with your life, but when you take your giftedness and align it with God's purpose for your life, you live the most powerful life for kingdom service.

The way we help people find their *sweet spot* is by helping them discover their God-given S.H.A.P.E.—an idea Rick Warren introduced to Saddleback Church in 1990. This idea was later explained in detail in Erik Rees's book *S.H.A.P.E.: Finding and Fulfilling Your Unique S.H.A.P.E.* I highly recommend this book for anyone in charge of ministry in his or her church. The accompanying small group study guide is a wonderful tool for guiding small groups through the discovery process.

Each of the five letters in the word S.H.A.P.E. represents a specific characteristic in your life:

S—*Spiritual gifts*. What are you gifted to do?

H—*Heart*. What passions do you have?

A—*Abilities*. What do you naturally do better than others?

P—*Personality*. How has God wired you to navigate life?

E—*Experiences*. Where have you been and what have you learned?

When you start asking people what they are gifted to do, their first response is very often, "Nothing," or "I don't know." The S.H.A.P.E. tool helps them explore their past, answer questions about their likes and dislikes, and discover what unique experiences they have had that prepare them for ministry. All too often the word *ministry* scares them away and they fail to realize God has been preparing them, every step of the way, for a unique servanthood opportunity specifically for them.

As your people answer these questions and look at the path of their life, they will begin to see how truly unique they are and discover how to use their S.H.A.P.E. in ministry. Ephesians 2:10 tells us that God sees us as his masterpiece: "For we are God's masterpiece. He has created us anew in Christ Jesus, so we can do the good things he planned for us long ago" (NLT). Not only do your people have something to offer, but they have something *unique* to offer. "God specifically designs each of us for doing his will on earth. Each one of us is intentionally shaped to fulfill the specific plan he has for each life. Understanding this amazing concept should produce in us a desire to humbly and gratefully accept the role God has created us to fill."[3] The people of your church need to know that if they do not fulfill their role, no one else will. It is specific to them; they have been placed in their church to make a specific and unique contribution. If they do not, the church will suffer as a result. "God has given each of you a gift from his great variety of spiritual gifts. Use them well to serve one another" (1 Pet. 4:10 NLT).

At Saddleback, we provide two venues for discovering S.H.A.P.E.: members classes and small groups.

### Members Classes

Members may take our 301 C.L.A.S.S. This is part of our C.L.A.S.S. system (Christian Life and Service Seminars), which gives our members the cognitive side of the five biblical purposes. The classes and their descriptions follow:

101—This basic introduction to our church family is designed to clearly explain to prospective members who and what our church is. Participants learn about our beliefs on salvation, our statements of purpose, and our church's strategy and structure. We also tell them about the history of our church, how the five biblical purposes are necessary to fulfilling God's calling for their life, and the plans for the future of Saddleback. At the end of this course, participants are given the opportunity to decide whether to complete the membership process by filling out and signing the membership covenant.

201—Participants are assisted in developing the habits they need to nurture spiritual growth. It provides an overview of daily time with God (quiet time, prayer, and Bible study), giving, and fellowship.

301—This class introduces participants to the S.H.A.P.E. concept and walks them through the process of discovering their unique S.H.A.P.E.

401—Participants are assisted in discovering their life mission and
how they can be part of God's plan to reach out to the world.
Participants in this class are taught:

> how to develop a personal perspective of the gospel message
>
> how to develop a personal story of how God has worked
> in their life
>
> how to build confidence in sharing their story
>
> how the P.E.A.C.E. Plan works and how they can be part of it

### Small Groups

The second way we encourage members to discover their S.H.A.P.E.
is through their small group. By using Erik Rees's six-week study,
S.H.A.P.E. Small Group Guide, small group members can have an
extended time to explore their S.H.A.P.E. in detail and also have a
built-in system of accountability in their small group. For example,
let's say a small group goes through the six-week S.H.A.P.E. study and
all of the members commit to try out a service opportunity of some
type. The following week at the regular group meeting, members will
naturally ask each other about their progress. Once a small group
member commits to becoming involved in a ministry, they have a
group of people who can encourage them in following through with
that commitment.

In order to encourage small group members to become and stay
involved in ministry, it is important that leaders remember to share
the ministry load. Have you ever played basketball with someone
who receives an inbound pass, dribbles the ball down the court, and
shoots it without ever passing the ball? We have a name for people
like that: *ball hogs*! They never work within a team environment;
they play for themselves.

I know many small group leaders who are *ministry hogs*. They do
all the ministry of the small group instead of sharing it and developing group members. It may be because their small group ministry is
designed around the leader doing all of the work, or it may be that
they have leadership issues and believe no one in their small group is
capable of doing ministry. The challenge for the small group point
person is to coach the small group leaders on how to construct the
group in such a way that the members become active participants who
are involved in not only developing their giftedness but also helping
others in the group to do so as well. The healthy small group is not

a classroom in which participants sit and listen to the leader teach from a Bible study. Instead, a healthy small group is a community of people who challenge each other to become all that God destined them to become. Every person in the group (both members and leaders) must be challenged to step out of their comfort zones and into the sweet spot of their giftedness. If you can help the people in your small groups experience service in a small way (a crawl step), it will change their lives forever. In order to do that, however, you've got to get the ball into their hands from time to time.

*A healthy small group is a community of people who challenge each other to become all that God destined them to become.*

A way to encourage people to use and develop their S.H.A.P.E. within the small group is to set the expectation of *purpose champions* for every group. We advise our small group leaders to let different people in the group take the lead in helping the group live out the purposes of the church (worship, fellowship, discipleship, ministry, and evangelism). This cannot happen, however, if your small group leaders are *hogging the ball*.

Without a system and structure such as this to balance the five purposes (holistic discipleship), a small group can easily overemphasize the purpose that expresses the gifts and passions of its leader and miss out on the other four. So what can you do to prevent this? You don't want to downplay the leader's strengths. Instead, it is important to acknowledge and use the strengths of the other group members as well.

Small group leaders can learn how to observe the strengths and areas of interests of the group members. Are there certain biblical purposes they get excited about? Do they enjoy hosting the group in their home? Are they enthusiastic about researching which study to do next? Is someone always willing to pray for the group? Is someone always encouraging the group to get involved in church projects? How about practical matters? Does someone always remember everyone's birthday? Is someone great about sending out emails or posting Facebook reminders to the group?

In my small group, Gina has the gift of hospitality and organization, so she keeps us on track socially. We often say that if she wasn't around, we wouldn't do anything. A perfect example is our group's annual winter trip. Gina's gift-set enables her to be tenacious in talking with and emailing our group to make sure the event happens. Of course she doesn't do it all, but she ensures we make the commitment—and we are always glad she did.

As your leaders consider the strengths of their group members, it will start to become obvious who should fill the roles of the different purpose champions. You don't need to use the title *purpose champions*, or any title for that matter. The idea is to find the passion of group members and give them the authority to run with that passion.

Developing purpose champions in your small group does two things: (1) It helps your groups become more balanced and healthy because you will have people focused on each of the purposes. (2) It makes people feel valued. You can get people in the game who might never have had an opportunity otherwise. Instead of one leader dominating the group, there will be five or more leaders who are all being challenged with developing their gifts and leadership ability.

Following is a description of the typical duties that might be under the leadership of the individual purpose champions:

*Worship*—This champion may lead the singing in the group, choose songs for the meeting, or delegate these tasks to others. This person may also oversee the prayer ministry of the group, lead in Scripture reading, and handle other similar activities. Think out of the box, though, and don't just look for someone who is gifted at singing. Some groups may never use music at all. Worship can be expressed in other ways, such as prayer walks, candlelit readings of Scripture, communion, and foot-washing ceremonies.

*Fellowship*—This person usually coordinates meals or refreshments for group gatherings. He or she may be responsible for organizing celebrations or parties (such as Christmas or birthday parties) and planning other social activities. This individual might also be just the one to start the group with fun icebreakers or even choose games for a game night.

*Discipleship*—People who are passionate about discipleship naturally encourage others in the formation of spiritual habits, so this champion can help ensure the group has a balanced spiritual diet. He or she can encourage group members to take a periodic Spiritual Health Assessment and develop a Spiritual Health Plan (see chapter 10) to make sure they each have a spiritual next step they are working on. This person may also help group members partner up for one-on-one accountability relationships as well as help them grow deeper in the spiritual disciplines. The discipleship champion may want to look deeper into study topics, bring additional materials to group meetings, and encourage attendance in various classes your church offers. This champion is always looking for your next step.

*Ministry*—This champion can help the group find opportunities to serve together within the church (believer to believer). He or she may also coordinate meals and support for group members in crisis (sickness, death in the family, birth of a new child, and so on). Ministry champions ask group members questions such as: What is your S.H.A.P.E.? Where are you going to use it? Have you attended 301?

During the 40 Days of Community, we assigned each group a project to work on together. We discovered that a group that does a project together, regardless of what the project is, builds a bond that holds them together. In 40 Days of Purpose, we had a 68 percent retention rate among the small groups that started. In 40 Days of Community, when groups participated in a project together, our group retention rate increased to 86 percent. Were there other factors? I'm sure there were, but clearly having a project to do together was a big one.

*Evangelism*—This person oversees outreach plans and helps the group partner and participate in mission projects personally, locally, and globally (believer to nonbeliever). Each of these three areas of outreach has a different target group, and I will touch on each one separately.

1. *Personally*. The champion encourages group members to ask: Who is next? Who am I going to pray about so I see him or her in heaven? Who are we going to assimilate into our group? The evangelism champion encourages group members to share with the group the story of how they came to accept Christ as their personal Savior. Once they are comfortable sharing their story with each other, they are encouraged to share it with others. The evangelism and fellowship champions might work together to plan a social event such as a cookout for people in the neighborhood so that nonbelievers can see Christians in an environment other than small groups or church.
2. *Locally*. The champion encourages the group to look at their community and determine where the most urgent needs are. Every area, no matter its size, has serving opportunities. Some local serving projects for groups at Saddleback include:
   After-School Club—serves elementary students by helping with homework assignments, reading skills, and other projects

Homework Club—provides tutors to assist young students on a weekly basis

Camp Pendleton Military Outreach—ministers to military families

Elderly Outreach—seeks to minister to the elderly and disabled by offering them time spent in fellowship, prayer, and worship

Breakfast Together—cooks and serves breakfast and leads Bible studies for people living in motels

Jail Ministry—reaches out to inmates by providing a church service

Urban Arts Outreach—builds relationships with the younger generation through creative arts

Manna—provides the needy with a means to purchase affordable food to meet their physical needs and creates opportunities to provide spiritual food through the love of Jesus

Recycling Ministry—collects items from church members to be recycled and then uses the money earned to purchase Bibles for people in other countries

City of Compton Outreach—provides opportunities to work side by side with churches and businesses in Compton by helping families improve their homes

Juvenile Hall Ministry—demonstrates Christ's love to teenage boys at a youth center through providing Sunday services, helping with homework, and organizing a game night

3. *Globally.* The champion encourages members of the group to be part of a global mission trip. This doesn't mean the whole group has to go; not every group is in a stage of life to be able to go on global trips. But every group should be able to mobilize a *home team* (those who stay and pray) and an *away team* (those who go on the trip).

When we first introduced the idea of purpose champions, as you might guess, not all of our small group leaders were on board immediately. Here is the story of one group that enthusiastically jumped in:

When Saddleback first started promoting the idea of balancing the purposes, my wife and I (relatively new believers) had only been leading our small group for about two months. We went to a meeting explaining this new concept and readily jumped on board. In retrospect, we didn't even realize this was new to Saddleback and just assumed it was how all of the groups were organized. Naively, we just jumped in and assigned purposes to group members. This immediately led to a flurry of activity as each member now felt the group was their group and their particular purpose was vital to the group. In retrospect, this was a huge change for the entire group. It completely opened our group up in terms of the types of activities we engaged in and assured that all of those activities were purposeful and not just social. Not only did we all experience a new level of spiritual maturity as individuals, but we also grew as a group.

So don't let your small group leaders become ball hogs. Get everyone in the game and watch as your groups are energized and new leaders emerge. Keep in mind formal titles might scare people away, but your personal encouragement to do the roles will involve people. People grow the most when they are serving and taking responsibility. Every task, no matter how small, is an opportunity to serve, show value, and develop people.

### Go: Help Them Serve by Providing Specific and Multiple Opportunities for Service

Several years ago we did our first 40 Days of Purpose Campaign. The campaign focused on a different purpose every week. During the ministry purpose week, Rick stood before our congregation and said, "If you want to serve, say, 'Here I am. Use me.'" Well, it turned out it wasn't quite that easy. Let me explain.

I'm not into numbers, but during that week God blessed us with about 2,200 people who said, "Here I am. Use me." The pastors gathered together in a room the following Monday and said, "Wow! What are we going to do with all of these people?" Rick looked each of us in the eye and said, "Harder on you, easier on them." Our job was to help them find ways to serve. We felt like we had just walked into an orchard where the fruit had just fallen and more fruit was about to fall. Do you know what happens to fruit that falls to the ground and isn't picked up? It rots; it spoils.

As you look around your church at all of the *ripe fruit*—people who want to serve others—how can you make it easier for them to get involved, even though it might be harder on you? There are many gifts that cannot be utilized in a weekend worship service. Where are those people with the gift of mercy? How can they use their gifts in the Sunday morning service? How about people with the gift of hospitality? Most often they don't really have the opportunity to use that gift on Sunday morning. But in a small group, these gifts can be used not only to serve each other but also to start exploring ways to use them in the church.

Here are some practical suggestions for your small group leaders to provide the kind of environment that will encourage people to use their gifts for service.

*1. Give authority with responsibility.* When you ask people to be purpose champions or fill some other role, give them the authority to get it done, and then let them do it. Don't constantly second-guess them or be looking over their shoulder. They may surprise you and do it better than you could!

*2. Utilize the power of asking.* Sometimes we think people aren't willing to serve, but the truth is that very often they have never been asked to do a specific task. Encourage your small group leaders to ask each person in the group to do something. Teach them to think small. Instead of asking a group member to be the worship purpose champion, the leader might ask him or her to bring a favorite song for the group to listen to as you close in prayer. A few weeks later, the small group leader might ask that same person to collect prayers from the group (perhaps on index cards) and commit to praying for group members during the week. The idea is to consider each person's S.H.A.P.E. and look for ways to slowly incorporate that into the group. If you do not teach your small group leaders to do this with intention, they will very likely end up doing everything themselves. "And let us consider how we may spur one another on toward love and good deeds" (Heb. 10:24).

*Don't let your small group leaders become ball hogs.*

*3. Motivate people to service through encouraging them.* I have found most people don't volunteer without being asked. A perfect example is Mark from my last church. He had it together with work, family, and church. At the age of forty-one, he was financially set. His social time was filled with his family, friends, and lots of golf. One day during lunch we were talking about some possible ways he could make more of a difference in the kingdom with his life. I posed a simple challenge: "Give me one golf game a month." I asked him if he would be willing to sacrifice the time it took to play one golf game a month (about five hours) to make room for more kingdom work. My Catholic background taught me how to use guilt, so I added, "One golf game for Jesus." Mark just smiled and agreed to let me know. A few days went by before Mark called me and said I could have one game a month. He ended up giving more than five hours, and he became a community leader. But none of this would have ever happened had I not asked.

4. *Always think incrementally.* Teach your small group leaders to apply the crawl, walk, run stages. Eventually, after the small group member has completed a few crawl steps and then a few walk steps, the small group leader can ask him or her to *run* and serve as a purpose champion. That person is much more likely to say yes if the leader points out the member would just be doing the same sort of things for the group he or she was already doing the last couple of months. The key is to start slow and give the person a chance to succeed in little things before asking something big (in task or title). It is a principle you can use in developing your leaders and that you can also teach them to use as they develop the people in their groups.

*Take time in your group meeting to honor those who have served.*

5. *Share serve stories.* Teach your small group leaders to take time to share *serve stories.* Give group members a chance to share their stories and tell of their experiences serving. Sometimes just hearing someone else's story will inspire others to become involved in serving. Take time in your group meeting to honor those who have served. Your groups might even want to take on an annual project of honoring selected volunteers in some way. Perhaps they can pool their money and offer to pay for dinner and a babysitter on some Saturday night. Or they could just show up at a volunteer's house and rake leaves or shovel snow from their driveway.

6. *Use small groups as a way to introduce people to service in a nonthreatening way.* People who are hesitant to serve individually are often more willing to serve as part of a group. Serving as a team in a small group builds memories and relational depth. An individual might not sign up for a Habitat for Humanity project, but if the entire group signs up, the person will feel more comfortable serving with a group of people he or she knows.

### Show: Help Them Feel Appreciated by Showing Your Gratitude throughout the Year

It is not enough to *tell* your people you appreciate them—*show* them. A Gathering, Appreciation Event, Small Group Night, Connection Rally, or whatever you want to call it brings together all your small group leaders (current and future) under one roof so they can see the big picture beyond their individual small group. Current leadership consists of those doing the small group ministry, from those working the infrastructure to those leading the groups—anybody and everybody who plays a part. Future leaders are those who are going to play a role in the future but don't know it yet.

*Future leaders are those who are going to play a role in the future but don't know it yet.*

So how do you determine who to invite for future leadership? A couple weeks before the event, ask all of your existing leaders to answer the question, "If you were to be gone tomorrow, who would do your role for the church?" That is the person they invite to the Gathering. If they don't know *who*, which is the case more often than not, encourage them to think and pray about who to ask.

People need to feel valued and to know they are part of something important. A Gathering reinforces your church's vision and the value of small groups. At Saddleback, we do two Gatherings a year, one in the late summer to get the groups ready for our fall campaign and another one after the holidays in January or February to get our groups out of the holiday funk. Our infrastructure has gotten so large that in the summer we do a Gathering for our community leaders (our infrastructure that oversees all of our over 3,500 adult small groups) and one for small group H.O.S.T.s (leaders).

Here is what a Gathering can do for your church:

- unite people under the same focus
- cast vision repeatedly
- reaffirm *why* they do what they do
- honor them and show value for what they do
- connect them with others in similar positions
- align people behind a common vision and goal of the pastor
- help them see what part they play in that vision
- give people a chance to see their leaders up close and personal and to hear from their hearts and ask questions

- pull people together and create a sense of shared ownership in the vision
- recruit new volunteers
- empower your leaders, which allows newbies to see leaders take hold of the vision
- instill discipline and motivation to carry the vision forward because people will sacrifice for a vision but not a task
- fuel the vision through motivation and inspiration, alignment and direction
- produce excitement through a demonstration of community
- show the authenticity and integrity of the leadership
- begin to teach your leaders how to think out of the box

So once you decide a Gathering is a good idea, how do you organize it? Following are some practical suggestions based on what we have learned at Saddleback. Although your small group ministry may be different in size, most of the same things need to be done.

1. Set a date. We all need a deadline in order to get anything done, and a Gathering is no exception. Avoid major holidays and other church events.
2. Make sure the date works for the senior pastor and ask him or her to speak. This puts the senior pastor in front of the core leadership of the church.
3. Make sure the date chosen falls at a time that provides optimum impact for the launch of small groups.
4. Have good worship and a flow that has energy, heart, and a message.
5. Provide food or dessert; do not make it a potluck. Whenever possible, invest in your leaders.
6. Include costs for the Gathering in your small group ministry budget. Your choice of how you spend your money shows what you value.
7. Emphasize the importance of the group leaders' contribution. Everyone has 168 hours a week. Make sure they know their hours are needed, because if you don't, something else will creep in.
8. Use word-of-mouth advertising. It is important to put your Gathering in the bulletin, mailers, email, social media, and so forth, but the best invitation is a personal invitation.

9. Keep creative, fresh, and new by building on a theme. It doesn't have to be expensive and an art festival, but building a theme keeps your message in front of your people.

10. Include personal recognition in the program. It costs you nothing to recognize people—the youngest, the oldest, the longest doing group life, the newest leader. . . . You get the idea. Think of reasons to highlight them. Be sure to recognize spouses of leaders—they are often the unsung heroes.

11. The more personal the better. Create low-key and high-spirited events; sizzle fizzles. Let your people see you as authentic and enthusiastic by focusing on the tenor and tone of the presentation.

12. Have them take an action step. What do you want them to do with what they hear at the event? At least, let them know of upcoming events.

13. Follow up on their action step after the Gathering is over. At Saddleback, we follow up with the guests each leader brought in order to find out if they want to be part of the ministry.

14. Send all participants a personal thank-you note for coming or save the postage and place thank-you notes at the tables instead of place cards.

15. Celebrate after the event. Gather the team who planned the event and debrief on what worked, what didn't, and how you might improve the event next year.

You may be thinking, my church isn't as big as Saddleback, so do I really need to do a Gathering? Bottom line—yes! If I had five groups, I would do a Gathering in my home and have them bring up-and-coming leaders. Basically, I would do everything I do for thousands but scale it down. Have a party. Feed them. Have some fun. Cast some vision for the upcoming year. Whatever you do, make sure your people feel appreciated and needed.

## Questions

Do the people of your church understand they each have a unique contribution to give to the church and the world at large?

_____

_____

_____

What methods do you use to help them explore their gifts, their
S.H.A.P.E.?

_____

_____

_____


Once your people have discovered their gifts or S.H.A.P.E., what system
do you have in place to allow them to try out serving opportunities?

_____

_____

_____


Do you have short, low-bar, _crawl_ opportunities for people to try
out serving?

_____

_____

_____


Do you have service opportunities for your small groups to do as an
entire group?

_____

_____

_____


Do you have multiple service opportunities you make known to your
small group members?

_____

_____

_____


How do you celebrate servanthood?

_____

_____

_____

Do your small group leaders understand their role in developing others, or are they there to merely lead the group through Bible studies?

_____

_____

_____

# 8

## The Church with No Walls

*Opening the Doors of Your Church*

[The Great Commission:] Then the eleven disciples went to Galilee, to the mountain where Jesus had told them to go. When they saw him, they worshiped him; but some doubted. Then Jesus came to them and said, "All authority in heaven and on earth has been given to me. Therefore go and make disciples of all nations, baptizing them in the name of the Father and of the Son and of the Holy Spirit, and teaching them to obey everything I have commanded you. And surely I am with you always, to the very end of the age."

Matthew 28:16–20

This [Great Commission] was given to every follower of Jesus, not to pastors and missionaries alone. This is your commission from Jesus, and it's not optional. These words of Jesus are not the Great Suggestion. If you are part of God's family, your mission is mandatory. To ignore it would be disobedience. You are the only Christian some people will ever know, and your mission is to share Jesus with them.

Rick Warren

My son, Ethan, is a special needs kid. When I take him to the playground, my prayer as his dad is always the same: "God, would you help him connect with some kid? Any kid. I don't care who it is. Just let him connect with some kid so they can play together." I sit at a picnic table and watch my child navigate the playground. Honestly, it can be brutal. To see him rejected, or worse yet ignored, really hurts me. I remember times when he came home from kindergarten and said, "Daddy, they said I'm different." As his dad, who loves him more than anything in the world, it just kills me to hear this. Watching it from a picnic table on the playground is even worse. So I sit there and pray that he will connect with someone and won't be alone on the playground. Fortunately, more times than not God has answered my prayer and given him someone to play with. But there have been painful times when I had to sit and watch him in isolation while others played nearby.

Now let's change the playground a bit. Let's call the playground your *church*, your *small group*, or *where you hang out*. And now it is not me watching, but your heavenly Father. He has sent some children to your playground. Maybe they are a little different from you. Maybe you aren't comfortable around them because they don't act the same way others do. So you just ignore them. Or perhaps they are in your neighborhood, or you see them in the store or the gas station as you go about your daily activities, and you ignore them or outright reject them. Now imagine God watching and saying, "Please connect with him. Reach out to her. Connect with my beloved child." Can you imagine the pain God must feel as we walk by, right past his child?

*Can you imagine the pain God must feel as we walk by, right past his child?*

## The Tension between Fellowship and Evangelism

Evangelism is difficult for many of us. Consistently, when people are asked which of the biblical purposes is most difficult for them, they say *evangelism*. Yet we often ignore this fact in our churches. Don't let the tension between fellowship and evangelism become the elephant in the room. Talk openly about it; if possible, from up front. If you are a lead pastor, address it through your sermons. Discuss the implications of people not finding community.

We all want evangelism to happen. The question is *how*. This tension isn't a sin; it's reality. How we address it is just as important as how we do it.

### Evangelism in Our Fractured Society

We live in a fractured society. It is common for families to be scattered across the country due to demands of their jobs. I have three older brothers and an older sister; each one of us lives in a different state. Getting together as a family takes a lot of planning and traveling for everyone. As a result, it doesn't happen as frequently as we would all like. If you have three children and send them all off to college, the chances are very slim that all three will be able to come back to their hometown and find employment. Even if you live in a major city, the competition in the job market often forces people to move several states away for their career. The U.S. Census Bureau reports the average American moves 11.7 times in a lifetime.

In addition, divorce has become commonplace. The most frequently cited statistics state that somewhere between 40 and 50 percent of all marriages will end in divorce. As a result, children are often forced to split their time between two households, sometimes traveling to different cities or even different states for visitation. As a result, many of us are growing up without a strong, positive role model of family or true community. We are starved for community and seek experiences and situations that make us feel grounded and part of something. It is not too much of a stretch to imagine that a small group can provide this type of community. Fellowship, and the relationships it develops, fills a need. I know many group members who say they are closer to their small group members than they are to their blood relatives.

*Don't let the tension between fellowship and evangelism become the elephant in the room.*

In contrast, evangelism is often uncomfortable. When you gather a group of Christians together and encourage them to meet weekly for a year and form strong bonds, it should be no surprise to learn that once they find community in a small group, they are reluctant to invite newcomers into the group and risk losing this sense of community. In addition, birds of a feather flock together. Many Christians will tell you they don't even *know* any non-Christians beyond the grocery store clerk or gas station attendant, and it is a bit difficult to strike up a meaningful conversation while buying groceries or paying for gas. While it may be a bit of an exaggeration to say that most Christians don't know any non-Christians, research has found that once a person becomes a Christian, his or her circle of non-Christian friends decreases dramatically.

### How to Open the Doors

So how do you get people to reach beyond their comfort zone, open the doors of evangelism in their small group, and reach out to non-Christians?

1. Admit the tension between fellowship and evangelism. Don't bury it under the rug. Talk about it; discuss the implications and how they can be addressed.
2. Define *evangelism* clearly. Tell the people of your church what it is and what it isn't. Let them know exactly what you (and God) expect from them.
3. Have a plan for starting new groups so you do not disrupt community in existing groups. It's easier to start a new group than break up an existing group.

### Define and Set Clear Expectations

It's important for the people of your church to understand evangelism from a biblical perspective. It's time for them to drop the often negative connotations associated with evangelism—the person standing on the corner screaming about the return of Jesus, or the pushy Christian who offends people with their "witness." Instead, we need to understand how evangelism fits into God's overall plan.

Evangelism is sharing the Good News of the gospel of Jesus Christ with those who don't know him. Evangelism has eternal significance and is the only one of the five biblical purposes that you can't do in heaven. If you can do evangelism on the other side of life . . . well, you have a problem! So let's do it on this side. It involves the privilege of working with God and representing him to others. It is telling your story. In John 9, after Jesus heals the blind man, he simply tells his story: "I was blind but now I see" (v. 25). Just tell your story.

Finally, evangelism is a duty all Christians share. It is not optional; it is required. As Christians, part of the way we worship God is through telling others about him. "But I count my life of no value to myself, so that I may finish my course and the ministry I received from the Lord Jesus, to testify to the gospel of God's grace" (Acts 20:24 HCSB).

Once you begin to define evangelism as something that is relational and tell your people their job is to simply share their story—not convert people—then they begin to move the focus away from their discomfort and toward obeying God. Think incrementally:

*Crawl.* Share your story in the small group.

*Walk.* Invite someone over for dinner without talking about church or Jesus to build a relationship.

*Run.* Share your story with the people you have built a relationship with.

When people begin to accept the concept of relational evangelism and realize they can just relax and be themselves, they are more willing to step beyond their comfort zone. For far too long we have allowed Christians to ignore God's Great Commission for personal evangelism. We have motivated by guilt instead of helping people be relational. Some people are certainly more gifted at evangelism than others, but evangelism is not a matter of giftedness—it is our legacy.

## Methodology

When I was in seminary taking classes on world missions, one thing my professors stressed repeatedly was that if we want to bring the gospel to other cultures, we need to be sensitive to those cultures. We should focus on biblical principles, which are true in every culture. But we need to be flexible and sensitive to the fact that American methodologies don't necessarily work in other cultures, and vice versa.

In my early years of leading small group ministry, I forgot that lesson from seminary. I read all the books on cell groups, metagroups, house groups, and anything about community in general. All those books from churches around the world and in the United States taught generally the same methodology—start a group and then after a certain amount of time, divide the groups and multiply into new ones. In essence, the books all advocated building community for a short period of time and then disrupting community to create more groups, and thus evangelism could happen.

For years I tried to teach that, push that, beg for that to happen, all with the same results—a very small percentage would heed my leading. My goal was for the groups to multiply, but all they did was divide—against me! Now, it could have been an issue with my leadership. But when I talked with the people in other churches, they were having the same problem. Even when I talked to people in the trenches of the churches about which the books had been based, I heard about the same types of problems. What sounded good on paper wasn't working in the day-to-day life of small groups.

Even knowing all this, I continued to try to make it work because that's what the books said to do. But finally an old tape in my head from seminary kicked in. What was the principle and what was the methodology? And where did the methodologies come from? I did some research and realized most of the American small group influence was coming from Korea, China, and Colombia. Their methodology worked well in their cultures, but in American culture it didn't work. The principle (evangelism) wasn't wrong; they birthed groups in order to see evangelism happen. I want the same principle to happen here at Saddleback Church—evangelism, and aggressive evangelism at that. But their methodology simply did not work for our church. Why was this a struggle for our church, and the American church in general?

In order to answer that question, I looked at what I had been learning about my culture. In doing thousands of Spiritual Health Assessments, I learned the majority of people scored low on the purpose of evangelism. It just wasn't a strength in comparison to the other four biblical purposes (fellowship, discipleship, worship, and ministry) found in the Great Commission and great commandment.

*Small group point persons are dying on the hill of believing in a principle while totally missing correct methodology for their culture.*

So we have a culture where Christians score low on evangelism, divorce is ripping families apart, and generations of Americans are moving away from their families to follow career paths. When you look at these three factors, it is no surprise very few of the people in my ministry were willing to give up the sense of community they had found within their small groups. Yet all across America small group point persons are dying on the hill of believing in a principle while totally missing correct methodology for their culture.

Let's agree: we want to do evangelism in our small groups. Let's also agree that if birthing groups out of existing groups works in your culture, that's awesome. But if it's not, let's also agree that we need to figure out how to accomplish evangelism in the context of small group life in a way that's a cultural fit.

At Saddleback Church, we have adopted a methodology that has helped us take our small group ministry from 280 adult small groups to over 3,500 adult small groups over the last twelve years. Since 2004 we have been running a higher attendance in small groups than in our weekend services. How has this happened? What is our methodology for ensuring evangelism takes place?

*Thinking like a farmer, we **harvest** seasonally and at specific times.*

We have found two things to be true: (1) It is far easier to start a new group than to get an existing group to multiply. I learned to avoid division by stopping talk of multiplication. (2) It is easier to empower a new person to start a new group with a couple of friends than to place the individual in an existing group of people he or she might not know (or like). We call this the Two Friends Rule. If you have two friends, you can start the journey and begin a group. If you don't have two friends . . . well, uh . . . there might be another issue that should be addressed.

### Starting New Groups

Our primary strategy for starting new groups is our *campaign strategy* (see chapter 17 for more details), which is something we do once a year, usually for six weeks in the fall. Thinking like a farmer, we *harvest* seasonally and at specific times, but we also do the ongoing work (planting, watering, weed pulling) fifty-two weeks of the year. Before the campaign, we ask our existing groups for volunteers who will step out of their group during that time to lead a new group. At the end of the six weeks, the volunteer can then either turn leadership over to someone else in the group and go back to his or her original group or stay with the new group and continue serving as H.O.S.T.

During the campaign we align the five learning modes around a central, compelling question and implement it throughout the church, from the children to the adults. The five learning modes are these:

1. *Ears.* Some people learn through listening, so we want people to attend the weekend services.
2. *Mouth.* Some people learn through discussion, so we encourage them to participate in a small group.
3. *Mind.* Some people learn through memorization, so our small groups do Scripture memory.
4. *Hands.* Some people learn through doing, so we have our small groups do a service project together.

5. *Eyes*. Some people learn through reading, so we have people do a daily reading.

Each of these five learning modes is centered on a theme that all small groups are doing churchwide. Everyone is on the same page, with a similarly themed sermon series and delivery of additional materials through the small group system. Roll these factors together and the result is exponential growth and alignment in your small groups. If you don't have small groups, this strategy is the perfect way to begin them. If you do have small groups but they all seem to be going in different directions, this is the perfect way to align them. If you are starting a small group ministry, read the article at www.smallgroups. net/start.

### Groups for Life?

One of the things I am often asked is how long we allow our groups to continue meeting. If they want to, we let them go on for life. We don't tell them that ahead of time; we let them discover it. Letting your groups focus on building community helps instill some natural by-products. First, it helps them see that you care about their spiritual health and their community needs. It also builds trust and opens communication for you to teach personal evangelism in a safe way that won't disrupt community in the process.

Remember, however, that even though we don't divide groups, we still encourage people in the groups to do personal evangelism. So if they don't add people to their group but still effectively do personal evangelism, then it is a win/win. Also, my experience has been that even when you don't plan to add people to the group— you do. People move, schedules change, life stages change. Many factors influence the dynamics of the group. Whatever the factors are, a group has two options: either it will dwindle to nothing or it will organically grow.

### Buh-Bye

Campaigns can work on a very practical level as well. Because we launch groups for life, it can be difficult for an individual or a couple to leave a group. One of the great things about having a campaign and asking for volunteer leaders is it gives people permission to leave. It can be awkward to say, "You know what, it's time for us to leave."

Instead, we give them the opportunity to say, "Hey, I would stay with you, but Pastor Rick has encouraged us to go and start a new group. We've been thinking about this, so we're going to make the sacrifice and leave this group."

After a campaign, some volunteer H.O.S.T.s will stay with the new group and some will return to their original group. Very often when people lead a group for the first time, they develop bonds with the group very quickly and it is difficult for them to leave those people and go back to the original group. During the 40 Days of Community, my small group was able to start four other groups. During the campaign we continued to meet in our own small group on Tuesdays, and then we met with our new groups on Thursdays. After the campaign ended, those four new groups continued and most of us came back to our regular group. One couple in our group bonded so well with their new group that they decided to stay. Here is Eric and Vicki's story:

> It's hard to believe that six years have passed since my husband and I stepped up to lead a small group during the 40 Days of Community Campaign. I can remember Rick Warren encouraging all of the members to step up as hosts. At first we did not respond to the call because we were already comfortable in our small group. Besides, even if hosting was as easy as "turn on the video and serve food," inviting people was overwhelming to me. I always worried about those awkward excuses and the abrupt *no*. I must say God worked quickly and changed my husband's and my hearts.
>
> We volunteered to be hosts, and as soon as we registered online, my next-door neighbor sent me an email inquiring about the 40 Days Campaign. This was amazing! I wasn't aware that they were interested in our church. It turns out their daughter had been going to Saddleback Church's high school ministry. They had come to a service to check things out, and that is when they heard about the campaign. From there it got easy; I invited more friends, and they invited friends, and so on.
>
> Today this group still meets. It has grown and changed and we've rotated leadership, but the core group is still intact. The most amazing thing about being part of this group is being a witness to how Christ works through his people.

When they came to us and said, "We feel God is calling us to stay with this group," we blessed them and said, "This is great, you go for it." They are still leading that group today.

## Group Size

We also do not try to control the size of our groups. We never want to penalize people who are natural gatherers. Certain people start with a group of eight and in no time they have twenty-five or thirty people gathering in their home—all trying to arrive early so they will have a place to park their car and a chair to sit in. Instead of discouraging these gatherers, we teach them to *subgroup* (see figure 8.1). Subgrouping ensures that everyone gets a chance to share. In groups larger than eight, it is very easy for quiet members to sit silently while the more vocal members monopolize the conversation. A group of thirty people can still get together and spend some time in fellowship at the beginning of the meeting, but then they subgroup into four or five smaller groups for discussion. Some groups can move to the dining room or kitchen while others meet in the living room or go to the basement. They are only limited by the number of rooms in the house. Then after the discussion time, they can come back together as a group or dismiss on their own.

**Figure 8.1**
**Group Meeting**

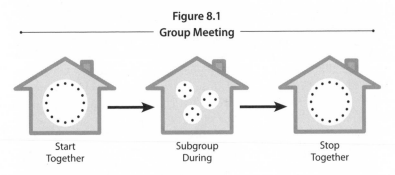

| Start Together | Subgroup During | Stop Together |

## Quantity versus Quality

Whenever you talk about evangelism, whether in the church at large or in small groups, you will hear two challenges. First, some people are going to think all you care about is increasing the size of your church. They will say, "All you care about is numbers. God doesn't care about numbers."

You have to be prepared to respond, "Who says God doesn't care about numbers? In the Old Testament there is a book called Numbers! So maybe he cares about them a little more than you think he does." Okay, maybe you shouldn't say that. But you can help them understand that although the focus is not on numbers, numbers are still important because every number represents a soul.

The second thing you are going to hear is, "We want quality people, not quantity." The thing is, however, that quality and quantity do not have to be enemies of each other. You can have both.

Let me give you an example: Let's say Lisa and I go camping and we lose both our kids somewhere in the forest. If you've been camping with us, you know that is not out of the realm of possibility. But for now, let's just say it's a story. We have lost both of our kids. Lisa goes north to look for them; I go south to look for them. We plan to meet back at the tent in one hour. When we meet up, Lisa has found one of them and I am empty-handed. We don't say, "Oh, let's go home. We found the quality one."

To our heavenly Father, each one of us is a *quality one*. That is the vision you want to drive into the hearts of your people.


## Close to Home

Let me tell you some of my background to give some insight into why I have a passion for evangelism. I was not born into a family of believers. We were Catholic by name, but we didn't know Christ; we attended Mass purely out of duty. Ours was a moral home, but we didn't have Christ as the center. That changed after my older sister, Nita, was invited to a small group in which she experienced the love of Christ through the group members.

She then brought that love of Christ home to our family. One by one, she began working on each of us. My parents became Christ followers at the age of fifty-four. I remember my mom asking, "Where were all of the believers while we walked around in the dark?" Evangelism became her passion. Soon evangelism became a natural part of not only her life but my father's as well. I remember one time a repairman came to our house to work on something, and before my mom gave him the check, she shared the gospel. That's not quite my style, but I am certain God used her. My dad was a bit more subtle, sending Christian tracts along with his checks in monthly bills and leaving his Bible on his desk at work.

Now, one thing everyone appreciated about my parents was that they knew how to throw a party, and I loved those parties. Before they were followers of Christ, their parties centered on alcohol, and I learned how to make and serve drinks. After they became followers of Christ, the parties were about community. I still served people drinks, but after these drinks people could still drive safely. My parents threw two huge parties a year, inviting Christians and non-Christians so the people not following Christ could see believers having fun. It was a true Matthew Party (Matt. 9:10, "While Jesus was having dinner at Matthew's house, many tax collectors and 'sinners' came and ate with him and his disciples").

So when did I join the family of believers? I will never forget the day Nita asked me if I wanted to become a follower of Christ. It blew me away. We were upstairs in the den watching a show on the Jesus Movement of the 1970s. I wanted her to draw the fish or PTL symbol on my arm like she had drawn on her own. She asked me if I knew what it meant. Of course I didn't; I just wanted it on my arm. It looked cool. What a perfect lead-in for my sister to start sharing. I was in junior high when that question led to a conversation that started my journey with Christ. In our den, my sister and I both fell to our knees, and she prayed and led me to the Lord.

I wouldn't be in my current ministry without the three girls in Nita's small group. What if those girls had not invited my sister to a small group? What if they hadn't stepped out of their comfort zone and shown her the love of Christ? Where would I be right now? I certainly wouldn't have written this book, and you wouldn't be reading it.

I also have three brothers. They had moved out of the house by the time of Nita's conversion. As I write this, two of them know the Lord through the constant prayers, conversations, and modeling of parents who wanted to make sure their sons will be in heaven. And my third brother says he is closer than I know. My parents couldn't rewind the tape and raise us in a Christian home, but they did their best to share the gospel with their sons. Nita is currently on staff at a church in Wisconsin, helping in their recovery and small group ministries. I will forever be indebted to her and that small group for showing me the love of Christ.

## Questions

Are you a good role model for evangelism?

_____

_____

_____

Who are you trying to reach?

_____

_____

_____

With whom are you sharing your story?

_____

_____

_____

On the spectrum between valuing evangelism and valuing fellowship, to which side do you lean? What can you do to create a healthy balance between the two in your groups?

_____

_____

_____

What plan do you have in place for multiplying new groups?

_____

_____

_____

What plan do you have in place for dealing with the problem of groups that are getting too large?

_____

_____

_____

Do the people of your church see evangelism as an act of worship? If not, what are some ways you can begin to share that vision?

_____

_____

_____

9

# More than Music

*Worship in the Life of Your Groups*

Since we are receiving a Kingdom that is unshakable, let us be thankful and please God by worshiping him with holy fear and awe.

Hebrews 12:28 NLT

The heart of God loves a persevering worshipper who, though overwhelmed by many troubles, is overwhelmed even more by the beauty of God.

Matt Redman

Do you think of worship as the latest CD in your car? Is it just the first part of your weekend church service? What does worship look like in a small group? Worship is more than music. It is anything that brings pleasure to God. How do you encourage your small groups to experience true worship? If you want your groups to have these *God moments*, you will have to guide them in the right direction.

## Hide-and-Seek

My kids love to play hide-and-seek. When they were very young, they thought if they hid partially behind something and then covered *their* eyes, we couldn't see them. So Lisa and I had fun with them and played along. When we came across them with their face in a chair and their whole body sticking out, we said something like, "Where can they be? I don't see them anywhere!" Of course then they would giggle, making their hiding place even more apparent. Eventually we would *find* them, and the game would start all over again.

*Adults like to play spiritual hide-and-seek.* I have found that hide-and-seek is a game many of us never relinquish. Adults like to play spiritual hide-and-seek. The goal is to keep people from finding out who we really are and what our struggles are. When you play that kind of a game, you don't let anyone *see* you, and you become dependent only on yourself. It is a game that can be played on two levels: hiding from others and hiding from God.

When you hide from God, you become quite adept at compartmentalizing your life. You act and speak a certain way in church, where you know God and his people can see you. When you are in the community, however, maybe at work or while playing golf with your buddies, your language and actions are very different. At home, perhaps you are a third person. And when you are alone, you do things you don't want *anyone* to know about. Of course you are never really alone; God is always with you. But very often we act as though we can hide from him. We give him specific areas of our lives but keep control of others, refusing to surrender them to him.

The heart of worship is daily, ongoing surrender of all areas of your life to God. It is as simple, and as complicated, as that. You must choose to surrender your attitudes, your actions, your thoughts, and your words to God and live *one* life in front of him, the church, the community, your family, your spouse, and most importantly, yourself. In order to do that, not only are you going to need an ongoing dialogue with God through prayer, but you are also going to need to have people in your life with whom you can share your struggles. As the point person for small groups, you need to have these things in place in your life and then encourage the people in your small groups to do the same.

Have you ever done that exercise where you fall back and trust someone to catch you? When my daughter, Erika, was eleven, we had a talk about trusting God. To give her an example of trust, I told her to stand in front of me and fall back into my arms. Of course as her daddy, I would never let her fall, but I also assured her that at 6'4" and about 240 pounds, I was more than capable of catching her seventy-pound body. The key in this exercise is for the person to fall back completely, keeping both feet planted and resisting the urge to step back to stop the fall. It took Erika a couple of falls with catching herself before she finally fell back into my arms. It was a great lesson in trust. When you trust God and fully surrender to him, he will always catch you.

## The Necessity of Support

If you are in ministry, you are a huge target. Unless you have support to build your reliance on God, you are not going to make it. We all need one or two people we can connect with on a very deep level. We also need a small group of people with whom we can share our life. The question is, who is that for you? Who are you turning to for support and guidance? To whom are you revealing your struggles? Who is going to be beside you when life gets tough? Do you share your problems with your small group, or do you show up every week and pretend to be Super Christian? When you, as the leader, admit you aren't a Super Christian and are dealing with your own struggles, you give others permission to do the same.

One of the things pastors say is that the problem with a living sacrifice is that it keeps crawling off the altar. I'm sure you can relate to that; I certainly can. I've made lots of commitments and surrendered lots of things to God through the years, but there have been times when I haven't followed through. You may hear a message at a camp or retreat that moves you, and you make a renewed commitment or surrender an area of your life. Often, though, you get back home and don't share your plans with anyone else, and you soon get off track. None of us are strong enough by ourselves to keep our commitments. If I am going to stay surrendered, I need to have some people in my life who help keep me on the altar.

## Helping Your Groups Connect with God

Following are some brief, practical ideas for helping your small groups connect on a deeper level with God:

*Encourage spiritual partners in your small groups.* Ask your small group leaders to instruct their members to find spiritual partners within the group. Train your leaders to encourage group members to share things they want to surrender and then help them develop a plan to do so. Set up your groups so this is done on a regular, ongoing basis. At Saddleback, we use the Spiritual Health Assessments and Spiritual Health Plans (see chapter 10) to do this. Model this behavior from the pulpit, during small group training, during small group events, and in all of your interactions with small group leaders. Then encourage your small group leaders to model it with their small groups.

*Prepare your leaders by enriching their minds and hearts.* Give your small group leaders good books to read for spiritual development such as *The Pursuit of God*, by A. W. Tozer, and *Desiring God*, by John Piper.

*Engage groups in the presence of God.* Have a night of worship to bring groups together for corporate worship. There doesn't have to be a sermon, but provide plenty of time to reflect on God.

Share *testimonies in weekend services of God moments.* Ask group members to share their testimonies in larger services. There is nothing more powerful than a story from the heart. Be professional but be real and share what God has done through the group.

### Basics of Worship in a Small Group

We have found it useful to think of group worship in terms of expressive worship and reflective worship. It does not have to involve music, but it needs to be more than just something to do. It needs to be an experience. Give your small group leaders a list of suggestions to pass on to their groups that doesn't just tell them to worship but also gives them practical suggestions they can use.

#### Expressive Worship

Following are examples of expressive worship for groups:

*Prayer.* Whether as a group or as individuals, make audible prayer a part of every small group meeting. That doesn't mean forcing each member of the group to pray out loud, but give every member the chance to do so.

*Thanksgiving.* Go around the group and ask members to say one sentence of thanks to God for something specific in their life.

*Music.* This can be low-volume music played in the background during prayer time or an all-out worship fest right in your living room. The idea is to do something that works for your group.

In our small group, John is our unofficial worship leader. Not too long after he started coming to the group, I learned he loves music and plays the guitar. When I chatted with him about his passions, I learned he likes to lead worship. But when I asked him to lead worship for our group, he said, "No, I'm not qualified." This is where most people start, never believing they are ready. But through some encouragement and leading (okay, pushing), John agreed to give it a try. His first time out of the gate was a bit shaky, but over time he has led us in some awesome times of worship.

John grew by taking a risk, but his willingness to step out in faith also encouraged another guy in our group to step out and lead worship too. Now do the two of them think they are the worship champions for our group? No. But are they the worship champions of our group? Yes. Every role in our group has started out like that. In developing roles, just think *crawl, walk, run.* Everyone starts by crawling, then gradually he or she begins to walk, and before you know it, that person is off and running.

Encouraging John accomplished a couple of things: (1) Our group benefits from John's gifts because he is really good at what he does. (2) John's increased involvement in the group gives him a sense of ownership. He feels like he's contributing and making a difference with the gifts God has given him. He may not know the Bible well, and he may not really know how to share his faith yet, but he knows how to worship and love God.

*Sharing struggles.* Encourage group members to share their struggles with the entire group. As they do so, be sure to stop and pray for each other.

*Sharing God stories.* Tell each other how God is working in your life. Such stories can be a great way of not only adding depth to your relationship but also worshiping God for all he is doing in your lives.

One of the stories I share is about when Lisa and I were thinking about moving to Colorado. Soon after we were married, it became clear to us that our ministry in North Hollywood was coming to a close. Since my parents had always taught me to pray specifically, and we were going to be making a change in churches, I told Lisa that if we had to move, we should pray for a desirable geographic location. So we pulled out a map and said, "Lord, if we have a choice, we would like to pray for a ministry opportunity in San Diego, the Bay Area in Northern California, or because we both like the mountains, the Rocky Mountains." Not feeling the Rocky Mountains was specific enough since they run across six states, we narrowed it down to Denver.

Less than thirty days later I received a call from a church concerning a job opening. They told me what a great opportunity this new position was, that their church was poised for the next move of God, that they were looking for someone like me who wanted to do ministry, and so on. I honestly wasn't paying too much attention until they said they were located in Denver, Colorado. My ears perked up and I asked them to repeat everything, because I was now listening with a different perspective. I agreed to explore the opportunity, and they agreed to send me an information package.

After I hung up with them, I quickly phoned Lisa and told her about the call. But we both quickly wondered if it was from God or just a coincidence. Later that week the information package arrived, and in it was a book the pastor, Charles Blair, had written, *The Man Who Could Do No Wrong*. In one section of the book, Blair writes about ignoring his wife's counsel on a certain situation. As a result, the church suffered a major difficulty. Well, I thought if it was good enough for him, it would be good enough for me too. So on Wednesday during lunch at Numero Uno Pizza in North Hollywood, I asked Lisa for her counsel. I asked her if there was something heavy on her heart about this potential move. If so, I wanted us to pray about it to see if this was God's leading. I fully expected her to say something about leaving her family, because they had lived for generations in the Los Angeles Basin and this move would be 1,000 miles away! Instead, her short answer was, "The snow." She was born and raised in Burbank, California, and was fearful about driving in the snow. So I said, "We'll pray about the snow," and we prayed God would calm her fears and make our path clear.

> *God stories are just that—stories about when the supernatural God intersects with our lives.*

That evening in Lisa's small group, for some reason the leader changed the normal study and decided to explore a Scripture that deals with fear: "When it *snows*, she has no fear for her household; for all of them are clothed in scarlet" (Prov. 31:21, italics added). Later that night Lisa shared with me what had happened. God or coincidence? Are you kidding me? Could God have made it any clearer?

God stories are just that—stories about when the supernatural God intersects with our lives. When Lisa had to tell her boss we were leaving, she was a bit nervous about bringing up the subject. As if to show God's sense of humor, when she approached her boss, he was wearing something that just had to be a sign from God—a Denver Broncos T-shirt!

### Reflective Worship

Following are examples of reflective worship for small groups:

*Silent prayers.* Take time to be still and listen. Give group members time to silently commune with God.

*Solitude moments.* Have a small group meeting during which members are asked to go away by themselves with their Bible for an hour. This can be done outside in a park setting or just in a home by allowing members to go to different parts of the house and then come back together and share with other members of the group. Or an alternative is to come back together for a simple prayer and then release members while they are still in a contemplative mood.

*Meditation.* Meditate on passages of Scripture. Perhaps provide group members with paper and pens to write their thoughts after meditation.

*Fasting.* Encourage group members to go on a two- or three-day group fast—whether from food or an activity. Be available to support each other during the week via emails and phone calls. (See www.smallgroups.net/fasting for a guide to fasting.)

### Confessional Preaching

If we want our people to be real, it has to start from the top. People are more endeared to us through our weakness than our strength. Pray for the lead pastor to use personal experiences in his messages so people can see him or her as a real person rather than up on a pedestal. If you have the opportunity to speak during the weekend services, be sure to do the same. You cannot ask your people to do anything you are not willing to do yourself.

Such sharing may reveal personal pain and suffering. We all handle pain and suffering differently, and unfortunately, I withdraw from others and tend to carry the burden on my own shoulders rather than letting anyone in. It's certainly not ideal for a small group guy, but that's the way I'm wired. When my son, Ethan, was young, Lisa began to sense his journey was going to be different from most. I listened, but I thought since Lisa tends to see the glass half empty, she was just overreacting. Unfortunately, not too long after we found out her discernment was right on target when Ethan was diagnosed with autism.

Lisa stayed on task. She began researching autism on the Internet and looking for ways to help Ethan. During that troubled time, she stayed focused and was the anchor that kept the family from drifting. I, on the other hand, continued to believe God would fix this. He had fixed so many other things in my life, and this was my beloved son. God had come through for me before, and I hung on to the belief that he would come through for me again. I would like to say it was my strong faith that sustained me during this period. The truth is that I tried to avoid even thinking about it. As reality continued to sink in, there were many times during those weeks when I fought back tears.

*If we want our people to be real, it has to start from the top. People are more endeared to us through our weakness than our strength.*

One day, right in the middle of a weekly meeting with my staff, the walls of Jericho tumbled down. The meeting started out normal (if you can ever call my team meetings normal), but somewhere along the way the pain just hit. I started crying—right in front of everyone. And I'm not talking about just a few tears sliding down my cheek but one of those uncontrollable, snot-dripping-from-your-nose cries. My staff froze, just looking at me in bewilderment with no idea of my inner turmoil.

As I dismissed the meeting and tried to pull myself together, someone on staff told me, "You need to buy what you sell. You need a support group." That started a journey of healing. Although we went to a support group just for parents of kids with autism, our small group and my staff played huge roles in an ongoing process in my life. Our small group has journeyed with Lisa and me through the pain, sometimes just listening and praying with us.

We all have our cross to bear. In our small group, each one of us carries a cross. Has God miraculously cured all of our crosses? No. Do I wish he would? Absolutely! But part of worship is surrender. I have had to surrender Ethan to the Lord. I wish the journey was different, but I trust the Lord and look forward to the other side where life is perfect. I also lean on Psalm 116:6 for Ethan, "The LORD protects the simplehearted; when I was in great need, he saved me." Remember, when you feel abandoned by God but continue to trust him, you worship him in the deepest way.


## Questions

Who is your spiritual partner?

_____

_____

_____

Do you meet on an ongoing and regular basis?

_____

_____

_____

Do you share your struggles with your personal small group?

_____

_____

_____

Are the meetings in your personal small group more about getting through the study or about worshiping God?

_____

_____

_____

Do you have a list of worship suggestions for your small group leaders? If not, begin to jot one down in the space provided below.

_____

_____

_____

What does God want you to surrender? We all have our personal crosses to bear. What will bring you closer to God as the point person for groups that will in turn bring you closer to your calling?

_____

_____

_____

# Step-by-Step,
# How Can I
# Do This?

## 10

# Spiritual Health Assessment

## *Living Life on Purpose*

Examine yourselves to see whether you are in the faith; test yourselves. Do you not realize that Christ Jesus is in you—unless, of course, you fail the test?

2 Corinthians 13:5

As a leader, the greatest gift you give people is who you are becoming in Christ. People follow you for who you are more than what you do.

Dallas Willard

### Spiritual Health Assessment

Before you can build your small group strategy, you have to realize the importance of working on your own spiritual journey. We all have a dark side—something *broken* inside us. If you are not aware that you need to work on your own issues, you are wasting your time. If you don't realize your spiritual journey needs to be engaged and developed, you are missing what being formed in Christ is all about.

Before you can guide your small groups in achieving balance, you must understand how to work on balance in your own life.

Like our physical health, our spiritual health needs to be assessed and managed. What does spiritual health look like? Some measure spiritual health by having the right answers to theological questions. Others believe spiritual health is demonstrated by acts of service. While these are good things, our spiritual life suffers if we do not balance all five of God's purposes in our lives.

In order to help people get a better sense of how well they're doing this and how they might develop a plan for improvement, we put together two tools we offer in a single booklet:

*Spiritual Health Assessment.* This self-assessment tool is designed to help people take a snapshot of their life and see how well they are balancing the five biblical purposes. The goal is neither to score high nor to compare oneself with others. Rather, we want to provide a starting point from which people can begin to pursue a healthier spiritual life.

*Spiritual Health Plan.* Once someone has completed the Spiritual Health Assessment and has identified a weak area, this tool will help him or her to develop an action plan for growing in that area.

Table 10.1

**Spiritual Health Assessment**

| Worship: You Were Planned for God's Pleasure | Doesn't Describe Me | | Partially Describes Me | | Generally Describes Me |
|---|---|---|---|---|---|
| How I live my life shows that God is my highest priority. | 1 | 2 | 3 | 4 | 5 |
| I am dependent on God for every aspect of my life. | 1 | 2 | 3 | 4 | 5 |
| There is nothing in my life that I have not surrendered to (have kept back from) God. | 1 | 2 | 3 | 4 | 5 |
| I regularly meditate on God's Word and invite him into my everyday activities. | 1 | 2 | 3 | 4 | 5 |
| I have a deep desire to spend time in God's presence. | 1 | 2 | 3 | 4 | 5 |
| I am the same person in public that I am in private. | 1 | 2 | 3 | 4 | 5 |

| Worship: You Were Planned for God's Pleasure | Doesn't Describe Me | | Partially Describes Me | | Generally Describes Me |
|---|---|---|---|---|---|
| I have an overwhelming sense of God's awesomeness even when I do not feel his presence. | 1 | 2 | 3 | 4 | 5 |

| | | | | Worship Total _____ | |
|---|---|---|---|---|---|

| Fellowship: You Were Formed for God's Family | Doesn't Describe Me | | Partially Describes Me | | Generally Describes Me |
|---|---|---|---|---|---|
| I am genuinely open and honest about who I am. | 1 | 2 | 3 | 4 | 5 |
| I regularly use my time and resources to care for the needs of others. | 1 | 2 | 3 | 4 | 5 |
| I have a deep and meaningful connection with others in the church. | 1 | 2 | 3 | 4 | 5 |
| I have an easy time receiving advice, encouragement, and correction from others. | 1 | 2 | 3 | 4 | 5 |
| I gather regularly with a group of Christians for fellowship and accountability. | 1 | 2 | 3 | 4 | 5 |
| There is nothing in my relationships that is currently unresolved. | 1 | 2 | 3 | 4 | 5 |
| There is nothing in the way I talk or act concerning others that I would not be willing to share with them in person. | 1 | 2 | 3 | 4 | 5 |

| | | | | Fellowship Total _____ | |
|---|---|---|---|---|---|

| Discipleship: You Were Created to Become Like Christ | Doesn't Describe Me | | Partially Describes Me | | Generally Describes Me |
|---|---|---|---|---|---|
| I am quick to confess anything in my character that does not look like Christ. | 1 | 2 | 3 | 4 | 5 |
| A review of how I use my finances shows that I think more about God and others than I do about myself. | 1 | 2 | 3 | 4 | 5 |

| Discipleship: You Were Created to Become Like Christ | Doesn't Describe Me | | Partially Describes Me | | Generally Describes Me |
|---|---|---|---|---|---|
| I allow God's Word to guide my thoughts and change my actions. | 1 | 2 | 3 | 4 | 5 |
| I am able to praise God during difficult times and see them as opportunities to grow. | 1 | 2 | 3 | 4 | 5 |
| I find I am making better choices to do what is right when I am tempted to do wrong. | 1 | 2 | 3 | 4 | 5 |
| I have found that prayer has changed how I view and interact with the world. | 1 | 2 | 3 | 4 | 5 |
| I am consistent in pursuing habits that are helping me model my life after Jesus. | 1 | 2 | 3 | 4 | 5 |
| Discipleship Total _____ | | | | | |

| Ministry: You Were Shaped for Serving God | Doesn't Describe Me | | Partially Describes Me | | Generally Describes Me |
|---|---|---|---|---|---|
| I regularly use my time to serve God. | 1 | 2 | 3 | 4 | 5 |
| I am currently serving God with the gifts and passions he has given me. | 1 | 2 | 3 | 4 | 5 |
| I regularly reflect on how my life can have an impact for the kingdom of God. | 1 | 2 | 3 | 4 | 5 |
| I often think about ways to use my God-given gifts and abilities to please God. | 1 | 2 | 3 | 4 | 5 |
| I enjoy meeting the needs of others without expecting anything in return. | 1 | 2 | 3 | 4 | 5 |
| Those closest to me would say my life is a reflection of giving more than receiving. | 1 | 2 | 3 | 4 | 5 |

| Ministry: You Were Shaped for Serving God | Doesn't Describe Me | | Partially Describes Me | | Generally Describes Me |
|---|---|---|---|---|---|
| I see my painful experiences as opportunities to minister to others. | 1 | 2 | 3 | 4 | 5 |
| | | | | Ministry Total | _____ |

| Evangelism: You Were Made for a Mission | Doesn't Describe Me | | Partially Describes Me | | Generally Describes Me |
|---|---|---|---|---|---|
| I feel personal responsibility to share my faith with those who don't know Jesus. | 1 | 2 | 3 | 4 | 5 |
| I look for opportunities to build relationships with those who don't know Jesus. | 1 | 2 | 3 | 4 | 5 |
| I regularly pray for those who don't know Christ. | 1 | 2 | 3 | 4 | 5 |
| I am confident in my ability to share my faith. | 1 | 2 | 3 | 4 | 5 |
| My heart is full of passion to share the Good News of the gospel with those who have never heard it. | 1 | 2 | 3 | 4 | 5 |
| I find that my relationship with Jesus comes up frequently in my conversations with those who don't know him. | 1 | 2 | 3 | 4 | 5 |
| I am open to going anywhere God calls me, in whatever capacity, to share my faith. | 1 | 2 | 3 | 4 | 5 |
| | | | | Evangelism Total | _____ |

*Transfer your scores to the Spiritual Health Plan.*

It is not difficult to use these tools by following these five steps:

1. *Take the Spiritual Health Assessment.* This assessment shown in table 10.1 is divided into five areas: worship, fellowship, discipleship, ministry, and evangelism. Under each area are seven statements pertaining to that area, for a total of thirty-five statements. For each statement, score yourself from 1 to 5, with 1 indicating "doesn't describe me" and 5 indicating "generally

describes me." For example, the first statement in the area of worship is: "How I live my life shows that God is my highest priority." After reading the statement, the test-taker circles the appropriate score. When all the statements are marked, add up the scores under each purpose. Let's say you take the assessment and end up with the following scores:

Worship: 16
Fellowship: 20
Discipleship: 24
Ministry: 19
Evangelism: 18

These scores indicate that worship is an area in which you would want to grow, while discipleship is an area in which you could contribute to your small group.

2. *Find the purpose(s) you want to work on.* In our example above, let's say you want to work on the area of worship.

3. *Choose a crawl, walk, or run step to get started.* Inside the same booklet that holds the Spiritual Health Assessment and the Spiritual Health Plan is a list of crawl, walk, run steps for each purpose (see figure 10.1). These suggestions correlate with every question in the Spiritual Health Assessment. Let's say you scored a 2 on the first worship statement: "How I live my life shows that God is my highest priority." Turning to the crawl, walk, run suggestions for worship, you find the recommended steps for that question:

> *Crawl:* Ask a friend or spouse to help you identify your main concerns. What changes do you need to make?

> *Walk:* Spend time reading through the life stories of some of the people in the Old Testament. Journal about the characteristics in their lives that demonstrated that God was a priority. What principles could you implement in your own life?

> *Run:* Make it a daily habit to reflect on your activities for that day. Journal or spend time in prayer over how you saw God in your daily activities. How are your priorities shaped by recognition of God's presence?

4. *Transfer the steps to your Spiritual Health Plan.* The plan shown in table 10.2 is a one-page tool for you to write down your crawl, walk, or run step for each purpose (or just the one purpose on which you scored the lowest). Start slow and

### Figure 10.1
### Crawl to Run

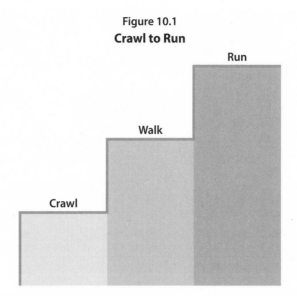

develop a plan that will work for you. Make sure you have a "what" and "when" in the "Practices" column. This helps your goal to be measurable and specific. Notice that in the "Partnership" column, you can select people you want to ask to help you with this particular step—they don't need to be your spiritual partners. This is the "who" of goal setting. Ever wonder who your mentors are? They are the people in this column.

Use the "Progress" column to record if you hit your target goal of the "when." Your spiritual partner is someone who helps you check up on the entire planner throughout the year.

5. *Find a spiritual partner.* In our example, let's say you choose the *walk* step for worship. You write down your plan in your Spiritual Health Plan and then show it to your spiritual partner. Taking it a step further, you might encourage your partner to also take the Spiritual Health Assessment and come up with his or her own Spiritual Health Plan for the year. Then the two of you can provide support, encouragement, and accountability for each other. The spiritual partner sees the whole planner but doesn't necessarily work with you on the individual goals of the planner.

Table 10.2

**Spiritual Health Plan for** _____ **(your name)**

I will share my plan with _____, who will be my spiritual partner to help me balance the five biblical purposes in my life.

| Purposes | Practices | Partnership | Progress |
|---|---|---|---|
| _What purposes are out of balance?_ | _What do I need to do, and when?_ | _Who will help me in this purpose?_ | _What progress have I made?_ |
| **Worship**<br>How I scored myself _____<br>How my friend **scored** me _____ | | | |
| **Fellowship**<br>How I scored myself _____<br>How my friend scored me _____ | | | |
| **Discipleship**<br>How I scored myself _____<br>How my friend scored me _____ | | | |
| **Ministry**<br>How I scored myself _____<br>How my friend scored me _____ | | | |
| **Evangelism**<br>How I scored myself _____<br>How my friend scored me _____ | | | |

Another feature of the booklet is the Friend Feedback Assessment. This assessment is exactly the same as the Spiritual Health Assessment page except the focus is on another person. For example, you give the Friend Feedback Assessment to a friend or mentor and ask him or her to score *you* on the statements under the five biblical purposes. It is often enlightening to discover how others feel we are doing in our spiritual walk.

For more information and to receive a copy of the Spiritual Health Assessment, Spiritual Health Plan, and Friend Feedback Assessment, go to www.smallgroups.net and click on *Resources*.

### There Are No Perfect Scores

It is important to understand this assessment is only a starting point and is not intended to cover every area of your life and faith. It is merely a way to begin thinking about how you can bring health and balance to your life. Also, remember that we will not be perfect this side of heaven, so don't grade yourself in terms of perfection. The assessment is to help you see where you might want to pursue growth and to point you in the direction of growth opportunities.

### Preparing Yourself for Assessment

I started using the Spiritual Health Assessment when it was still in the development stage in 1999. In the years since, the Lord has challenged me in many ways. I think you'll find the same challenges if you follow these three easy steps.

1. *Before you begin to take the Spiritual Health Assessment, pray!* Pray for an open mind to how the Holy Spirit wants to use this assessment in your life. This is not a test you take one time and then move on to something else. It is a living document that starts with the Spiritual Health Assessment and then provides accountability in the Spiritual Health Plan. As D. L. Moody said, "Discipleship is not in the information, but the transformation."

   *Remember that we will not be perfect this side of heaven.*

2. *Since this is a living document, think in developmental steps for the Spiritual Health Plan.* As you put down goals you feel the Lord wants you to work toward, think in the crawl, walk, run framework. For example,

the first year I took the Spiritual Health Assessment, I gave my best shot at the Spiritual Health Plan. The tool was still in the development stage, and we were testing it to determine what worked and what didn't. At that time we did not have crawl, walk, run steps, and I soon found my goals were too high, so I couldn't see any progress in the first month. Discouraged, I procrastinated on the very goals I felt the Lord wanted me to grow toward. So through the process of developing my own Spiritual Health Plan and failing to achieve my goals, I decided to develop a crawl, walk, run version of those same goals. Doing so helped me see progress as I conquered small, attainable steps along the way. Most of the time, people set goals too high and plan to attain them too soon.

3. *Share your Spiritual Health Plan with a few trusted people.* If no one knows what you have in your plan, it's easy to procrastinate. The devil seeks to defeat our plans by isolating us, but the loving community around us keeps us on track toward our goals. Also, understand that the planner is a living document; it will change throughout the year. The plans you set in January may look completely different in July. That's okay. As God works in your life, there *will* be change.

## Fresh Start

On the first Friday of every year, Lisa and I get together and share our personal Spiritual Health Plan for the coming year. In 1999, when my daughter, Erika, was just a baby, Lisa and I hired a sitter and went out and exchanged our plans over dessert. I looked hers over quickly and said, "Hey, this looks good," and returned the plan to her. She held mine in her hands and was still reading. I waited for her response. A few long minutes passed, and eventually she said, "I think there are some things that you're missing that are holes in your spiritual life and you should probably write them down here." So I said, "Oh? Can I have your planner back? Because I'm ready to be honest too." I can play this game!

As our conversation continued, one of the things she suggested I add to my planner was "develop family time." That is because a number of years ago I almost made a train wreck of our marriage. I fell more in love with my work than I was with my wife. We didn't have kids at the time, and we were able to work through it with some counseling. Since we had recently added a baby to the picture, Lisa wanted to make sure I did not fall back into my old ways of being a workaholic. So I added "develop family time" to my Spiritual Health Plan, and we finished dessert.

A few months later I was involved in a two-day conference at Saddleback. As I walked in the back door at the end of the first day, Lisa asked, "Hey, can you change Erika's diaper?" I barely broke stride and quickly replied, "Sure, babe. I just want to download a couple of thoughts from the conference first. I'll just go upstairs really quick and do that, and I promise you that in five minutes I'll be back down to change her diaper."

*Encourage your groups to think out of the box and perhaps even involve other groups in their spiritual next steps.*

Without a word, she walked over to the counter where my Spiritual Health Plan was and pulled it out. She opened it deliberately, pointed to a page, and said, "Two months ago, you vowed to me that you would work on this area. Your daughter is not an interruption in your busy schedule. If you want to be the spiritual head of this house and value your family, then you need to make a choice. Do you want to go upstairs or do you want to change her diaper?"

I felt like a sledgehammer had hit my chest. I mean, the wind was knocked out of me. I will never forget it.

I share this story at our Purpose Driven Small Group Conferences, and every time I tell it I have to choke back the tears. It still kills me.

Needless to say, I changed my daughter's diaper.

## Applying Your Assessment to Your Group Health

The Spiritual Health Assessment is a great tool designed for individual evaluation and health, and it can also be used as a small group tool to help the overall health and balance of a group. Encourage your group members to take an individual Spiritual Health Assessment and develop a personal Spiritual Health Plan. Once they have all scored themselves, suggest they get together and discuss how the group as a whole is doing in the area of balancing the purposes. Small groups can use the Group Health Plan (figure 10.2) to develop a snapshot of where their group is and then use the suggestions in tables 10.3 through 10.7 to develop crawl, walk, and run group opportunities for the five purposes. Encourage your groups to think out of the box and perhaps even involve other groups in their spiritual next steps.

First, use the top part of the Group Health Plan to write the names of the group members on the diamond according to where they scored high on the Spiritual Health Assessment. These names will get transferred over to the third column later under "Who Will Help?" After that, have the group work on the first two columns, "What Are We Doing Currently?" and "What Are Our Next Steps?" Go through each purpose and have the group write what they currently do in their group. You may write something or you may write nothing. That's okay; it's only a snapshot of where your group is at.

Next, use tables 10.3 through 10.7 to dream about ideas your group could do under "What Are Our Next Steps?" These should be goals your group could accomplish in the next six months. The Group Health Plan is found in the Small Group Leader Training Kit at http://www.smallgroups.net/Small-Group-Ministries-Store.php.

### Figure 10.2
### Group Health Plan

Discipleship

Ministry            Worship            Fellowship

Write the names of each
group member and their
area of strength to get a
picture of the health of
your group.

Evangelism

## Moving toward Balance

| Purpose | What Are We Doing Currently? | What Are Our Next Steps? | Who Will Help? |
|---|---|---|---|
| Worship | | | |
| Fellowship | | | |
| Discipleship | | | |
| Ministry | | | |
| Evangelism | | | |

Table 10.3

Worship

| Aspect of Worship | Crawl | Walk | Run |
|---|---|---|---|
| Prayer | Make it a point to pray for the group when you meet. You may want to open or close in prayer, but be sure you take the lead in making prayer a part of your group. | Have members of your group share specific things they need prayer for, and then pray for them. You may have one person pray for all the requests or have each member pray for one person. Be sure to keep a record of these prayers and ask about them on a weekly basis. | Take some time to lead your group through a time of structured prayer and meditation. |
| Singing Praise | Attend a worship service as a group and praise God together. | Invite someone to lead worship during your group time, or pick up worship DVDs from your local Christian bookstore. | Make singing and a time of praise a normal part of your small group meeting. You could sing a cappella, use the musical talents of members in your group who may play an instrument, or use a worship video/CD to help you worship together. |
| Communion Foot Washing | As a group, attend a worship service where communion is served. Spend some time in your next group meeting reflecting on how that time impacted each member. | Invite a leader from your church to your group to lead you in communion or a foot washing. | Lead your group or ask a group member to lead in a time of communion or foot washing. Make this a regular occurrence in your group. |
| Surrender | Get a study that focuses on ways to worship. What ways could you make this a practice in your group? | As a group, spend some time discussing things that each of you needs to surrender to God. Make it an open and confidential time of sharing your lives together. Commit to pray for those things that were shared. Spend some time taking communion together, remembering Christ's sacrifice of surrendering his life for you. | Agree as a group to fast together. It could be for one day or a specific time of day, and it could be from food or from something else. (Those with physical issues could fast from things other than food.) Spend the time together reflecting on your own dependence on God. Spend some time thanking God for all he has done for you and what he will do in the future. |

Table 10.4

Fellowship

| Aspect of Worship | | Crawl | Walk | Run |
|---|---|---|---|---|
| Building Community | | Celebrate significant occasions (birthdays, spiritual birthdays, etc.) as a group. Look for opportunities to play together. | Have an affirmation night where each person is in the "hot seat" while group members share what they appreciate about that person. | Go on a retreat together as a small group. This could be an affinity retreat (couples, singles, etc.) or a spiritual retreat. Carve out some time to be together. |
| Deepening Relationships | | Make prayer a central part of how you deepen your relationship with one another. Have a regular time for sharing concerns and requests and write them down in a journal. Refer back to the journal frequently to see how God has answered your prayers. | Take a night in between studies to go to dinner and/or see a movie as a group. Look for opportunities to spend fun time together. | Plan a weekend trip or go to a camp together. Look for fun ways to share life together. |
| Meeting Needs | | Take some time to pray for the needs of those in the group. You may want to write down those needs and check in with each other. | As people share their needs, look for ways that your group could rally around that person. There are some needs that we cannot meet, but make it a point to do everything you can to help each other. | Take the Spiritual Health Assessment as a group and discover each member's strengths. Then go through the Group Health Plan and have members meet some needs in your group based on those strengths. |
| Sharing Community | | To remind you that you are open to sharing community with others, write down the name of someone with whom you would like to do lunch or have coffee. | Get to know other small groups in your community. You may want to have a get-together with another small group to share together. | Invite someone new into your group. You may know someone you can invite, or you could talk with the leaders of groups at your church about who is looking for a group in your area. |

Table 10.5
Discipleship

| Aspect of Worship | | Crawl | Walk | Run |
|---|---|---|---|---|
| Curriculum | | For your next series, spend time talking as a group about what the next topic of study should be. Have people share what their needs are and what they feel would be beneficial to study at this time. Then choose a topic. | For your next series, choose a topic that you have never considered as a group to stretch you and make your group more balanced. If you always study books of the Bible, try studying a topic related to life stages or spiritual studies. If you always do topical studies, try studying a book of the Bible. Have fun expanding your horizons. | Plan your curriculum or topic of study a year in advance. Try to move to a place where your curriculum is balanced. Make a goal to do at least one study on a book of the Bible (discipleship), one study related to life stages (fellowship), one study on spiritual health/disciplines (worship), and one study related to outreach (evangelism/ministry). Make your curriculum reflect the balance you want for your group. |
| Accountability | | Have your group take the Spiritual Health Assessment. Ask each group member to share with one other person the area they have chosen to work on so they can pray for one another. | Take the Spiritual Health Assessment as a group. Have each person share their strength and the area they need to work on. You may want to have people pair up by gender based on strengths and weaknesses to mentor each other. (For example, if I am weak in evangelism, I should pair up with someone who is strong in evangelism.) Take the assessment on a regular basis (annually, biannually, etc.). | Have your group take the Spiritual Health Assessment and then walk through the Group Health Plan together. Look for ways to have group members take ownership of the group based on the strengths and passions they have for a particular purpose. Set goals for how you will balance the purposes over the next six months. |
| Spiritual Disciplines | | Have each member of your group connect with another person in the group for prayer support. Have people share things they would like prayer for, and make it a point to have those pairs ask each other about their respective prayer requests regularly. | Have your group share with one another the struggles they have in their lives and one way the group can help them to grow. You may want to have the men in one room and the women in another to allow for open discussion. Pray for each other's needs and follow through on helping group members to grow. | Take the results from each person's Spiritual Health Assessment and, based on their strengths and weaknesses, match people up in the group by gender as spiritual partners. (For example, if I am weak in discipleship, I should pair up with someone who is strong in discipleship.) This will allow members of your group to build into each other's lives in a natural way and not be seen as taskmasters trying to hold to a plan. Share the results with the group from time to time. |

Table 10.6

Ministry

| Aspect of Worship | Crawl | Walk | Run |
|---|---|---|---|
| Understanding Your S.H.A.P.E. | Do a study that explores how God has uniquely S.H.A.P.E.'d each person to serve. | Schedule some time to have someone from your church come to your group and share some of the ministry opportunities available based on the S.H.A.P.E. of your group members. | As a group, spend some time sharing each person's S.H.A.P.E. What are some ways that each member can contribute to owning the group, based on a particular purpose? Affirm and look for ways for them to contribute to the health of your group based on their passions for a particular purpose area. |
| Serving Your Group | Pick a way you can serve the members of your small group. You could wash a car for someone in your group, take care of the yard, or prepare a meal. Look for practical ways to serve each other. | Have each person in the group take on a role to help make the group better. Structure these roles around the purposes to help your group be balanced. Someone may want to handle the food (fellowship), handle prayer (worship), or trade off teaching (discipleship). Look for ways to include everyone so that each person can serve the group. | As a group, seek ways to serve other small groups. You may want to find out what the needs of another group are and try to meet them. Or you may want to offer to watch the children for a group so they can have a night out to build their fellowship together. Look for ways to connect with other groups in your area. |
| Serving Your Church as a Group | Take a night to serve the church by doing a simple project together, such as preparing a mailer to go out or preparing crafts for the children's ministry. | Take on a ministry event together as a group. You may want to volunteer to serve at one of the Easter or Christmas services. | Find a ministry that your group can support or serve in on a regular basis. Get a list of opportunities from your church and choose a way you can serve together as a group. |
| Serving Your Church with Your S.H.A.P.E. | Take some time as a group to reflect on the S.H.A.P.E. of each member. Have each person take turns being in the "hot seat," and have the rest of the group share the gifts and passions they see in that person. How could these gifts be expressed in ministry? | Have each person in your group take some time serving in one or two ministries in the church to get a feel for where they might best serve. | Encourage your group members to commit to serving in some kind of ministry at the church. Reflect regularly as a group about what God is doing in and through each person as they serve and celebrate God's goodness together. |

Table 10.7
Evangelism

| Aspect of Worship | Crawl | Walk | Run |
|---|---|---|---|
| Personal Evangelism | As a group, take a class on evangelism at your church. Spend some time discussing what you learned and how you could implement it in your group. | Identify three people whom you will pray for as a group, and make it a point to talk regularly about how you could invite them to your group. | Pick one person you will each share your faith with in the next week. Come back and report how it went. You may even want to invite the person to your group. |
| Group Evangelism | Have each person in the group pick the name of someone who doesn't know Christ in their neighborhood, and begin praying for those people. | Go through a small group study on evangelism. | Invite your friends who don't know Christ to a small group party to share a little about the community you have as a group. You may find that some of your friends want to attend your group. |
| Local Missions | Spend some time as a group mapping your neighborhood. Who doesn't know Christ? You could also identify those in your spheres of influence whom you could invite to dinner. | As a group, serve together in your local community. You could volunteer at a food bank or serve food around the holidays at a local mission. Go out for dessert afterward and take some time to share about your experience. | Choose to sponsor a need or cause in your local community. It could be a school, a mission, etc. Look for opportunities to serve through the missions ministry at church. |
| Global Missions | Identify an unreached people group that your small group will commit to pray for. Get more information about these groups from the missions team at church. | As a group, take a class on global missions at your church. | As a group, volunteer for a mission trip focused on the unreached people group you have been praying for. |

We have discovered many benefits from using our personal health assessment tool, including:

1. *It can give your pastor insight into how to lead the congregation effectively.* For example, if most of your congregation is struggling with evangelism, the pastor might do a message series on evangelism or offer a class about how to share Jesus with others. The assessment allows you to look at levels of issues that go a little deeper than what most people talk about.

2. *It promotes a sense of shared responsibility when it comes to spiritual health.* Offering an assessment reminds people that spiritual health is up to each of us—it's not the pastor's responsibility. The group score is an aggregate so that people don't compare each other, and it encourages them to see that they're not alone when it comes to spiritual growth.

3. *It gives people an intentional pathway for crawl, walk, and run steps.* The tool offers practical next steps for each of the purposes. For instance, if people score low in discipleship, there are suggestions for how they can build spiritual muscle in that area. This helps them plug into resources in the church and gets them thinking about movement, not arrival.

4. *It encourages people to serve out of their strengths.* By affirming people's strengths, it starts the process of organizing the church with intentionality. People mentor each other, and instead of focusing on weaknesses, accountability partners share their lives and learn from each other.

5. *It is an inspiration to set short-term goals.* We usually encourage people to take the assessment annually to check their progress and set short-term goals. It's a way to strengthen certain aspects of spiritual health over time.

6. *It is a tool to help grow healthy small groups.* This can be a great way for them to chart their spiritual health together. Again, the idea is not to look at individual scores but for group members to encourage each other and be accountable as they grow in Christ. When someone in the group shares that he or she struggles with evangelism and someone else says, "Me too," it's a moment for the whole group to learn and grow. If the group discovers that it is out of balance in that area, the members might decide to study a certain curriculum or try another crawl, walk, or run step.

### It's about Health, Not Size

Our major goal is health. We define success as balancing the biblical purposes. It is not about the numbers because you can have 100 percent of your people connected in small groups, but if those groups are not spiritually healthy, you do not have a healthy small group ministry.

Churches measure by attendance because it is easy, but is that right? It's much harder to measure the work of Christ in someone's life or discern whether a man is a better husband this week than he was last week. These types of measurements are not the easiest to measure, but they are the most important.

Rick taught me this saying: "People don't do what you expect; people do what you inspect." As you develop your strategy, you must have a way of *inspecting* whether your people are acting on the vision you have cast. Putting the tool in their hands so they might be able to self-inspect makes that tool even more powerful.

### Questions

How are you doing in the area of community?

_____

_____

_____

What is your spiritual next step?

_____

_____

_____

Do you have a spiritual partner with whom you have shared this next step?

_____

_____

_____

If not, who could you ask to be your spiritual partner?

_____

_____

_____

Which of the five is your biblical purpose?

_____

_____

_____

Are you fulfilling your purpose?

_____

_____

_____

How does your church measure spiritual health?

_____

_____

_____

What tool do you use to measure the health of your small groups?

_____

_____

_____

# 11

## Helping Groups Become Healthier

*Provide a Clear Pathway for Members to Follow*

> My steps have held to your paths; my feet have not slipped.
>
> Psalm 17:5

> People often complain about lack of time when lack of direction is the real problem.
>
> Zig Ziglar

### Think Developmentally

Your goal as point person of the small group ministry is to encourage your groups, and the individuals in those groups, to move forward along the path of spiritual maturity. How can you not only get them into a small group but also influence their growth while they are in that small group? How can you help your small group leaders encourage the people within their groups to also be moving toward spiritual maturity?

## Remove the Barriers

No matter what part of the country you live in, certain excuses for not joining a small group seem to be fairly common. It is important you know these excuses in advance and educate your small group leaders so they will have a ready response. In John 10:14 Jesus tells us, "I know my sheep and my sheep know me." Get to know the minds of your unconnected *sheep* and determine ways to help them get past their barriers.

These are the most common excuses you are likely to encounter:

*I don't have anyone to watch my kids.*

This is by far the top excuse we hear at Saddleback. The following are options we suggest our groups consider in addressing this dilemma:

1. Each family gets its own babysitter.
2. Use the homes of two members who live close to each other. Have childcare at one home provided by a babysitter or rotating group members and have your meeting at the other home.
3. Dedicate one room in the house for childcare and bring a babysitter to the meeting place. Each family can contribute money for childcare costs.
4. Rotate two members out of the small group on a weekly basis to provide childcare in another room of the house. In this way there will be no cost to anyone in the group. Be sure *not* to rotate out a married couple, but two husbands or two wives. This way, as they babysit, they get to know each other on a different level.

> *Get to know the minds of your unconnected sheep and determine ways to help them get past their barriers.*

5. Make your group a family group where children are allowed to play in the same room as the meeting. This works best when the children are very small and are not likely to catch much of what is being said. Such groups might even want to consider meeting in a local park.
6. High school students from the church might provide childcare as their ministry project. This is an excellent way to team up with the youth ministry and give teens a chance to serve. Check your state laws to ensure your church has no legal liability.

7. Trade childcare with another small group. If your group meets on Tuesday and you know of another small group that meets on Thursday, offer to watch their children while they meet and ask them to do the same for your group. This will remove the burden of cost.

We had this problem a couple of years ago in my own small group. We were making out our yearly Group Health Plan and determined that in the area of fellowship we were using childcare as an excuse to miss the group. This was especially tough on Lisa and me since with a special needs child we were paying thirty to forty dollars a week just for childcare. But we all agreed that if we believe this group matters, then nothing will stop us. The truth is, it boils down to a priority issue more than it does a childcare issue.

*I don't want to share my personal life with strangers.*

Many people have a fear of intimacy. They don't want to open up with others and risk the vulnerability that comes with honest and transparent relationships. To combat this, one of the strict rules you must drive home to your group leaders and group members is that what is said in the group stays in the group. People also need to know they will not be forced to share anything they do not want to share. It is important to let prospective group members know all they need to do is show up and get to know the other group members. They are not expected to join a group and immediately reveal all of their personal problems. As they move through the studies and begin forming relationships, the sharing will occur naturally.

*What is said in the group stays in the group.*

*I am not spiritual or very religious, so I wouldn't fit in.*

This is an excuse you hear from many new Christians, seekers who have not yet made a commitment to Christ, and even long-term churchgoers who have been content to just *pew sit* every week. People are afraid they will be forced to pray out loud or be put on the spot about issues in their lives. It is important to emphasize that small groups are places where *everyone* is looking for answers and that we can all learn from each other, no matter where we are on our spiritual walk. As the leader of your small group ministry (or as lead pastor), it is important to communicate this on an ongoing basis. Small groups are for everyone, not just the *Super Christians*.

*I don't have enough time.*

This is another frequent excuse. It is true, there are certain seasons of life when we have more free time than others. But the truth is also that we all have 168 hours per week. The question is, how are you going to spend your time? As a leader, your job is to help those in your influence to spend their time wisely.

*I don't know enough about the Bible.*

Many people are under the mistaken notion that they will feel out of place in a small group if they don't have a good grasp on the Bible. They imagine a group of people all reading from their Bibles as they themselves fumble through the pages trying to find Matthew. Your people need to understand that one of the purposes of small groups is *learning* about the Bible. No previous Bible knowledge necessary!

*I tried a small group once and didn't like it.*

Unfortunately some people have had a negative prior experience with a small group. Too often someone in their previous group betrayed a confidence, or they just didn't bond with other group members. Remind them that one bad experience does not necessarily lead to another one. Just because I have a bad experience at a restaurant doesn't mean I don't eat out again. Also give new people the opportunity to try out a group by allowing them to sign up for a four- or six-week study.

*I don't want to get into any sort of long-term commitment.*

Make sure people have multiple opportunities throughout the year to join short studies. Even if they do not stay with the group for the next study, the chances are they will join another study and eventually stay with a group for a lifetime.

## Group People by Affinity

If you group people by the things they have in common, they are more likely to want to join the group and are more likely to stay. Offer groups like these to your church:

*Common culture.* These groups share a similar language or similar stage of life.

*Common city.* These people live near each other—on the same block or in the same area of the city.

*Common calendar.* Give your members plenty of meeting days and times from which to choose. For example, we have some men in our church who are away on business trips most weeks, so they need a group that meets on weekends. Similarly, offer groups that meet during the day for stay-at-home moms whose children are in school.

*Common concern.* These groups build around certain family issues or social concerns in our nation or community.

*Common crisis.* This could be a health crisis, financial crisis, job crisis, and so forth. The idea is to start such groups to provide support and friendship.

*Common commitment.* This is for people who are committed to a particular ministry or project.

While these groups all gather under an affinity, the main goal is still balancing the purposes. They will be doing so, however, in a group of people drawn together by a common concern.

**Figure 11.1**

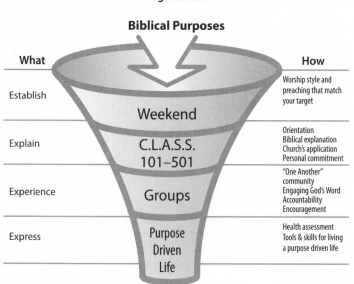

**Figure 11.2**

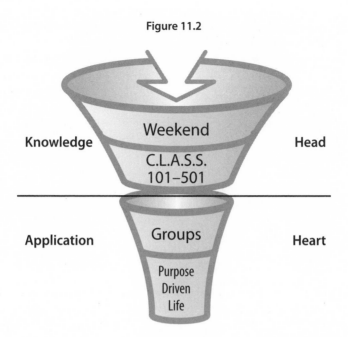

### The Acts 5:42 Process

We use another visual—a funnel—to depict how we increase participation and understanding of the five biblical purposes (see figure 11.1).

> *Establish*. We establish the five biblical purposes during the weekend services.
>
> *Explain*. We explain the purposes in our C.L.A.S.S. system.
>
> *Experience*. People experience the five biblical purposes in our small groups.
>
> *Express*. People express the biblical purposes in their everyday life.

Now look at the illustration of the Acts 5:42 Process in figure 11.2. Notice the line across the funnel between C.L.A.S.S. and Groups. Above the line (Weekend and C.L.A.S.S.) is *cognitive knowledge*—the head. Below the line (Groups and Life) is where the *application* takes place—the heart. Where so many churches go wrong is they preach about groups or they preach about the purposes and they have classes explaining them, but they don't encourage members to live below the cognitive line, in the area of the heart.

It is important that your people not only understand the purposes but also be continually exposed to them through small groups so they are eventually expressed in their personal lives. Don't stop above the line and merely explain the purposes. Give your people opportunities to live them.

## Questions

How does your church move people toward spiritual health?

_____

_____

_____

How do you move your small group members toward health?

_____

_____

_____

What are the excuses you hear from your people for not joining small groups?

_____

_____

_____

What solutions might you offer to those excuses?

_____

_____

_____

What types of affinities do you use to gather people?

_____

_____

_____

# 12

# Leadership Matters

## *Selecting and Recruiting Leaders*

If God has given you leadership ability, take the responsibility seriously.

Romans 12:8 NLT

Your highest calling is not to build your ministry, it is to passionately love and follow Jesus. And, the greatest gift you give those you lead is your own authentic walk with God. Too often we focus on growing the ministry organizationally instead of growing our leaders spiritually.

Lance Witt

It is the responsibility of the small group point person (or lead pastor) to set the vision and direction for small groups. In order to do this, I recommend going through Scripture with your team and developing a biblical philosophy of what it means to be in a small group and what it means to be a small group leader. It is important for you and everyone on your team to know *why* you are doing small group ministry.

### Develop a Clear Biblical Philosophy

When I first became involved in small group ministry, I held a romantic notion about the whole idea of community. It didn't take long for the romance to diminish and for reality to set in. I think this verse ought to be read at every orientation for small group leaders because it is realistic about group life and group leaders: "All those who were in distress or in debt or discontented gathered around him, and he became their leader" (2 Sam. 22:2). Every small group leader has had a group like that at some time. In fact there have been occasions when I think people who are distressed, discontented, and in debt are the only ones I lead. Why can't I lead the normal people? In fact, where *are* the normal people?

Somewhere along the journey of leadership, the path will become tiresome. Knowing the *why* will keep you from giving up and turning back. You are going to have difficult times when you wonder why you ever got into small group ministry and whether you are the right person for the job. There will be times when small group leaders won't return your calls. Groups are going to fall apart. People are going to question your philosophy and strategy. When you are directing a small group ministry, all kinds of problems will crop up because you will be dealing with people. If you could just have small groups without the people, it would be a breeze. But the fact is, you are going to be dealing with people, so it is going to be difficult at times. Unless your heart is in it and your motivation is strong and true, you are going to give up when the going gets tough. Knowing *why* you are doing small groups will give you a knot to hang on to when you are at the end of your rope. And helping your leaders understand the importance of their ministry will give them their own knot for a handhold.

*If you could just have small groups without the people, it would be a breeze.*

### The Value of Group Life

If someone asked one of your small group leaders, "Why does your church have small groups?" could he or she give an answer? How about the staff? What would they answer? How about the other pastors? Are they able to communicate the value of groups to others? It will be your job to carry this banner; it starts with you and moves through you to others. If you do not have a solid answer, don't expect anyone else to have one either. Consistent and frequent communication on the value of small groups is vital.

This is particularly vital with your small group team. Just as you must continually cast vision to the congregation, you must also keep the vision before your leaders. Don't ever assume that they have it. Repeat it during gatherings and meetings. Post it in the room where you meet. Print it on items leaders can place on their desks. Print it on a coin they can carry in their pocket. Make personalized T-shirts with a catchy slogan that captures your vision.

## Choosing Leaders

Once you and your leadership team are clear on *why* you are doing small group ministry, decide *who* will be your small group leaders. Begin by praying for emerging leaders in your church. As Christ tells us in Luke 10:2, "The harvest is plentiful, but the workers are few. Ask the Lord of the harvest, therefore, to send out workers into his harvest field." Where God guides, God provides. Everything starts with prayer. So pray, asking God to direct and lead you and to provide the leaders he has chosen.

Be open to his leading. What type of people are the best small group leaders? It isn't necessarily those who consider themselves great leaders. I love to hear about people who are somewhat reluctant to lead. They feel the nudging of the Holy Spirit, but they also feel a little hesitant and inadequate, and it's a little scary for them to step out. Those are the perfect leaders because they will be dependent on God. We want people to be open and coachable in training, so we appreciate people who are a little bit reluctant.

We look for certain characteristic traits that we have gathered together in the acronym F.A.I.T.H.

F—*Faithful*. Who are the faithful people in your church who are there day in and day out?

A—*Available*. Who has some time on their hands to give? Different seasons of life bring different demands. Look for people who not only have the desire to serve but also have the time.

I—*Inspired*. Who has a calling to ministry? Ministry is tough. When faced with obstacles, a person who feels called is more likely to stick it out.

T—*Teachable*. I have many rough edges, and some people in my life serve as *heavenly sandpaper*. Sometimes it gets tiring when they try to sand those rough edges off me. Sometimes it's painful, but it is always necessary. Look for people who are teachable, who are open to a little sanding here and there.

H—*Heart for God*. Do they have a heart and passion for God? If their heart is not in the right place, none of the other qualifications matter.

### Ask God for Suggestions

Right now, before going any further, think about the people in your church who have the characteristics of F.A.I.T.H. Close your eyes and give it some thought. As soon as you come up with a few names, write them down in the margins of this book. Now I encourage you to call or email them within the next twenty-four hours and tell them: "I was reading a book on small group ministry and I did an exercise on emerging leaders, and God brought your name to my mind. Would you consider going on a journey with me in small group ministry?"

*Look for people who are teachable, who are open to a little sanding here and there.*

I use this exercise during small group conferences and have had amazing results. One guy wrote back and said the following weekend he launched three new leaders because of this exercise. They were just waiting for somebody to ask. We have many diamonds in the rough in our churches, but too often they are missed because we don't put the spade to the soil and start to turn it over to find out who they are.

### Servant Heart

When you are looking for leaders, look for people who have the heart of a servant.

Do they have a willing heart? Will they do whatever it takes or just whatever is convenient?

Do they take initiative? Will they do more than what you tell them? Will they think of how they can apply new skills to their group?

Do they follow through? Can you count on them?

Are they willing to take on menial tasks? Leaders have to be willing to get their hands dirty. When Saddleback started, Rick literally did everything. He set the church up and took it down. He stored it in his garage. No task was too much!

Is their service motivated by love? First Corinthians 13:1–3 puts motivation in perspective:

> If I speak in the tongues of men and of angels, but have not love, I am only a resounding gong or a clanging cymbal. If I have the gift of prophecy and can fathom all mysteries and all knowledge, and if I have a faith that can move mountains, but have not love, I am nothing. If I give all I possess to the poor and surrender my body to the flames, but have not love, I gain nothing.

Do they celebrate others who serve? Are they jealous when others have a victory, or are they a champion for them?

### Fishing in Several Ponds

When you are looking for new small group leaders, think about fishing in several ponds. Start with the weekend services. Don't be afraid to ask people for this commitment during the regular services. I continue to be amazed when Rick steps up in front of our congregation and just clearly says, "Here is what I am asking you to do: ——. Will you do it?" People respond in unbelievable numbers. He doesn't beat around the bush and he doesn't soft sell it. He is straightforward and tells everyone exactly what we are looking for. It is amazing to see how people respond when they get that kind of clear call.

Beyond the services, think about elders and deacons, current ministry leaders, people with the gift of hospitality, and your current small group members (if you already have a small group ministry).

## Recruiting Leaders

Once you have identified potential leaders, recruiting them will often be the hardest task you face. We found that when we asked people to be a *leader*, a lot of them were intimidated and overwhelmed by the word, and so they often declined (we were asking for a *run* step). We then gave the word *shepherd* a try and didn't fare much better.

When Jesus recruited his disciples in Matthew 4, his first requirement was "follow me." Three years later it was "die for me." There is a huge gap between "follow me" and "die for me." Over the course of time Jesus raised the bar of requirements on the disciples. He didn't scare them off in Matthew 4 by saying "come die for me"; he started with a crawl step—"follow me"—and then developed them to a place of leadership where they would die for him.

We didn't realize it, but when we recruited our potential leaders, in their eyes we were asking them to "die for me." We should have been asking them to simply "follow me." We needed an entire paradigm shift, not only in understanding how our church members understood the word *leader*, but also in how we were projecting the image of a *small group leader*.

### H.O.S.T. Strategy

We simply could not find enough people willing to become *leaders* or *shepherds*. Finally, we changed terminology again and found the perfect fit. We asked people to become H.O.S.T.s, and they agreed in amazing numbers. By now you can guess that we have the letters in H.O.S.T. each represent something that gives a snapshot of what we are asking our people to do when they start leading a group:

H—have a heart for people

O—open your place (meet in a home, coffeehouse, restaurant, or workplace)

S—serve a snack

T—turn on the DVD

The very same people who said *no* to becoming a small group *leader* now agreed to be a H.O.S.T., even though the responsibilities were the same. Just changing the word from *leader* to *H.O.S.T.* made all of the difference in the world, and our number of volunteers soared. Following are elements of the H.O.S.T. strategy:

*The term* leader *is never used.* If the only people who ever lead small groups in your church are those with the gift of leadership, you will never have enough small group leaders. Even people who do have the gift of leadership may not recognize that gift in themselves. The idea is to remove the stigma attached to the word *leader* and simply ask people to H.O.S.T. a small group in their home.

*The bar is set very low.* Reducing the risk ensures more people will be willing to step out in faith and give hosting a try. Inviting a group of people into your home is not such a big deal. It is something we do socially all of the time. In contrast, *leading a Bible study* sounds like a huge responsibility to many people and is something they would never sign up for.

*Short-term commitment.* We don't ask them to stick with a group for the rest of their lives (though they might do just that). We ask them to invite some people into their home for approximately six weeks (depending on the length of the study). After that time period, they are done. No strings attached.

> *He didn't scare them off in Matthew 4 by saying "come die for me"; he started with a crawl step—"follow me."*

*Video curriculum.* We use video-based studies with competent and knowledgeable instructors providing content. Typically, the group gathers, chats for a few minutes, watches the video, and then goes through the printed material together as a group.

*Training included.* Before the group arrives, the H.O.S.T. may watch a short segment of the DVD that provides pointers and suggestions to get the group off to a good start for that session. These tips are called "Help for Hosts." Personalized instruction such as this is easily accessible and consistent.

*Printed curriculum with questions.* Our small group studies are economical and easy to use, and the H.O.S.T. does not need to come up with a study plan or questions for the night because they are already provided. This takes a great deal of responsibility off the shoulders of the H.O.S.T. and enables more people to feel comfortable leading a group.

*H.O.S.T.s are not introduced to any additional training unless they continue with a group.* Most groups will want to continue after the initial period. H.O.S.T.s who decide to continue are *then* introduced to the training they will need to develop their leadership skills. They will be walked through the process over time, incrementally, and through relationships with others in the small group ministry.

All of these aspects help the H.O.S.T.s to stay focused on loving the people God has put before them.

### L.E.A.D.E.R.S.H.I.P.

Once we have someone who has made it beyond the initial H.O.S.T. stage and has decided to continue along the Small Group Leadership Development Pathway (see chapter 13), we begin nurturing the characteristics found in the L.E.A.D.E.R.S.H.I.P. acronym.

L—*Listen to God daily*. If your leaders are not listening to God daily, how can they instruct their group members to listen to God? Your small group leaders need to model listening to God and meditating on his Word.

E—*Empower every member to share a group role or responsibility*. Good leaders develop the people in their influence. They don't lead a group of passive people; they lead every member into becoming an essential and valuable part of the group. Our H.O.S.T.s do this by encouraging members to become purpose champions through developmental steps.

A—*Authentically shepherd the sheep*. Your leaders must have the heart of a shepherd and see each person in their small group as someone within their sphere of influence and care. John 10:1–18 gives us a perfect description of authentic leadership.

D—*Develop a healthy and balanced spiritual life*. This is done through using the Spiritual Health Assessment and the Spiritual Health Plan.

E—*Engage in ongoing personal care and development*. Your leaders should be continually learning, and it is your job to provide them with learning opportunities. Most professions require some sort of ongoing education, so why would we even consider not providing ongoing education for our spiritual leaders? Our Small Group Leadership Development Pathway offers this continuing education.

R—*Release new potential*. The best leaders take seriously their commission to go and make disciples. They are always looking for ways to give the ministry away and are continually developing other current and potential leaders.

S—*Surrender their lives to Christ.* Once they have settled the question of their calling, your leaders will take on a new level of development. John 21:15 represents a pivotal stage in Peter's leadership. Once he could say he loved Jesus more than "these" (the 153 fish in the story, and his profession as a fisherman), then his ministry took off. A leader must make the choice to surrender his or her life on a daily basis.

H—*Humbly lead their group.* The example of Jesus washing the feet of the disciples is a great example of his willingness to do whatever, whenever. Once a potential leader is willing to do the most menial task for Christ, he or she is ready to do the greatest tasks.

I—*Invest their time in others.* The only way leaders can earn the right to speak into the lives of the people under their care is to spend the time to develop relationships with them.

P—*Pray consistently for their group.* My friends don't have to ask me for my prayer requests because they know my life and they know my battles. A great leader knows his or her people, and he or she knows their prayer needs.

### Qualifications

After a H.O.S.T. has decided to continue leading his or her group past the six-week timeframe, the bar is raised. Every church needs to establish minimum qualifications for a person to serve as a small group leader, so be sure you know what you are asking for and make it very clear. If it's your conviction, for example, that your leaders have to have been a believer for a certain amount of time or have to be a member of the church, state that from the beginning.

We give prospective leaders a one-page document at the conclusion of Leader Training 1 (see chapter 13), with our guidelines and leader values to which we are asking them to commit. Once they have read and agreed to these guidelines and values, we ask them to sign the document. Saddleback's minimum guidelines for small group leaders are:

1. Leader has accepted Jesus Christ as Lord and Savior.
2. Leader has completed C.L.A.S.S. 101 and is a member of Saddleback Church.

3. Leader has committed to completing all remaining C.L.A.S.S. seminars (201–401) within a reasonable period of time.
4. Leader has completed leadership training and agrees to implement the leader values listed below.
5. Leader is able to answer that there are no problems in the following areas:
   a. Leader has no current habitual struggles or moral issues (drugs, alcohol, cohabitation, etc.) that would bring shame on the name of Jesus Christ or on Saddleback Church.
   b. Leader has no current marital struggles (infidelity, separation, divorce in process, etc.).
   c. Leader supports Saddleback Church's statement of faith without any reservation or addition.

Saddleback Church's Leader Values:

1. I will commit, to my best of my ability, to live an exemplary Christian lifestyle while supporting the church's leadership and basic doctrinal statements.
2. I will commit to learning and growing through my daily time with the Father and other coaching/training opportunities provided by the church.
3. I will commit to developing a future H.O.S.T. and to cultivating a healthy and balanced group.
4. I will commit to including new members and releasing mature members to start new groups over time.
5. I will commit to seeking balance with both the great commandment and the Great Commission in my group.

The leader signs: "I meet the leader guidelines and commit to the leader values." Once they have agreed with and signed this document, they continue in our Small Group Leadership Development Pathway.

### Questions

What are the minimum requirements for a small group leader in your church?

_____

_____

_____

Do you have a crawl step for people to try out being a small group leader?

_____

_____

_____

What type of resources do you provide for your small group leaders?

_____

_____

_____

What type of support do you provide for questions or concerns they might have?

_____

_____

_____

# 13

## The Road Ahead

### *Developing a Simple Training Pathway*

> For this reason I remind you to fan into flame the gift of God, which is in you through the laying on of my hands. For God did not give us a spirit of timidity, but a spirit of power, of love and of self-discipline.
>
> 2 Timothy 1:6–7

> The ability to summon positive emotions during periods of intense stress lies at the heart of effective leadership.
>
> Jim Loehr

No matter what age we are—five, twenty-five, or fifty-five—none of us wants to fail. We always want to succeed; therefore our fear of failure is one of the enemy's most effective weapons. He uses it to keep us from following God's lead. It is one of the biggest reasons people do not step into a leadership role.

I love the verses from 2 Timothy that are quoted above, especially the critical phrase "fan into flame." As Paul writes to Timothy, he talks about doing something that will fan a spark into a flame. If you've ever gone camping and had to start a fire, you know that fanning a little bit of an ember is a key to having a roaring campfire.

Your desire to fan the leadership potential of your small group leaders into a mighty flame stands in sharp contrast to their fear of failing. As you prepare to stoke the ember, fear prompts them to do the opposite—kick dirt over it and hide it from view. As you uncover embers and nurture them along, do so slowly. Begin with just a whisper of breath. Tell them you believe in them, and just as importantly, let them know what is expected. Give them a clear pathway for training and easy access to resources.

## Training Tips

Based on my experience doing ministry at five different churches and trying a variety of things that worked as well as things that failed, here are my best training tips.

1. *Make training an expectation.* People who have made a commitment to become a small group leader need to be aware that training is a part of serving right from the beginning. You don't need to give all the training up front, but you do need to know where you are planning to take them. If they want to know the training pathway, share it with them.
2. *Make use of continuing education instead of giving all of your training to new leaders immediately.* Many churches require their small group leaders to attend multiple hours of training before allowing them to lead a small group. Instead, take an on-the-job approach. Once they start leading a group, they will quickly realize they need some more help to be effective. As a result, there is a much higher felt need and they are more willing to participate in training.
3. *Encourage training that is easily transferable.* Rick Warren has taught me that if you can't write your strategy on a napkin, it is too complex and won't be easily transferable. Your training needs to be simple enough for your leaders to understand where they are going and to pass the information on to others. Simplicity also ensures your training will not stop in the classroom but will be passed along informally from leader to leader.
4. *Make the training as relational as possible.* In the long run, relationships will be the most effective training tools you'll pass on to your leaders. If you can help them build relationships with each other and you, they'll always have a place to go when problems arise.

5. *Provide high-impact training.* Your people are too busy to attend poorly prepared training at your church. After they show up for one or two of that type of session, they are going to start voting with their absence. Provide training that is practical and makes an impact. Give them ideas and tips they can use the following week with their group. It doesn't have to be pretty, but it does need to be practical.

6. *Provide multiple delivery systems.* Don't be stuck in the rut of delivering all of your training in a classroom setting at the church. Look for various ways to deliver training. Some of our training venues include:
   a. classroom
   b. web-based training available as downloads or streaming
   c. interactive, web-based training (such as pairing a learner and leader via Skype)
   d. DVD-based packets to be viewed at home
   e. CD-based packets to be listened to in the car or at home
   f. community leader–based training, which tends to be more personal and can be held in a home, coffee shop, restaurant, etc.

7. *Schedule on-campus training around your service times.* Offer training before, after, or during services so your people are not forced to make an extra trip to the church during the week. If you have multiple services, think about setting up your training so your leaders can attend one service and then attend training during the following service. Make it as easy as possible for your leaders to receive training.

8. *Provide a notebook that feels incomplete.* Give them a notebook that will store the training materials from all your classes. At Saddleback we give our new H.O.S.T.s a three-ring binder that has a chart of our Small Group Leadership Development Pathway on the back cover. When they take Leader Training 1 (the second step on the pathway), we make it clear that they are expected to attend other classes. There are empty tabs in the notebook, indicating they don't have all of the information we want to give them. The notebook reinforces the expectation of continued training.

9. *Teach them to develop a team.* Leaders without a team are orphans; they are on the journey alone. One in five Americans relocate for jobs every year. That means 20 percent of your

church will be moving each year. Who will be ready to step into their role if they move out of the area? Teach your small group leaders to develop a team within their small group. From the beginning we tell our leaders, "Don't lead alone!"

10. *Take time to get their feedback.* As your small group leaders finish each training module, ask for their feedback. Let them know their opinion matters. Help them understand their honest opinions will improve the training for the next class.

## Core Values of Our Training Pathway

When we launched the 40 Days of Purpose Campaign at Saddleback in 2002, we started with over 3,000 people willing to be a H.O.S.T. We felt any weekend attendee who had accepted Christ could do that. Then we improved our on-the-job training for the months after the campaign. At Saddleback we call this plan the Small Group Leadership Development Pathway. It helps us fan into flame the leadership potential of our small group H.O.S.T.s. You may find this pathway helpful as you look at developing your small group leadership.

### Figure 13.1
### Small Group Leadership Development Pathway

"For this reason I remind you to fan into flame the gift of God, which is in you through the laying on of my hands" (2 Tim. 1:6).

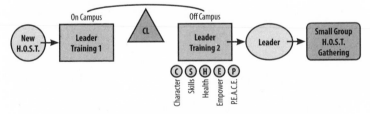

"And David shepherded them with integrity of heart; with skillful hands he led them" (Ps. 78:72).

The Small Group Leadership Development Pathway is directed by four core values that govern every aspect of our efforts:

1. *Leadership.* We believe leaders must continually be pursuing biblical excellence in their own life and leadership in order to properly impact those whose paths they cross.

2. *Relationship.* We believe encouragement, support, and accountability are vital ingredients to lasting spiritual transformation.
Therefore we strive to provide the right balance of coaching,
encouragement, and accountability.
3. *Stewardship.* We believe part of honoring God is honoring
who he has made us to be. Therefore we challenge all leaders
to discover and develop their God-given S.H.A.P.E. and use it
for his glory.
4. *Partnership.* We desire to learn the best practices within our
entire small group ministry, recognizing that greater success
comes through the sharing of ideas, talents, and resources.

As we take our leaders through the pathway, we seek to provide incremental training that not only will give them practical, hands-on advice
but also will instill these core values into the heart of each leader.

## Small Group Leadership Development Pathway

At Saddleback, the Small Group Leadership Development Pathway
is designed as a journey that replicates the one Christ made with his
disciples. We begin with a H.O.S.T. making a short-term commitment and end up with a robust leader who is ready to die for Christ.

### 1. New H.O.S.T.

When people become H.O.S.T.s, they start the journey of our pathway whether they know it or not. At this initial stage they have the
opportunity to lead a small group, but the bar is set very low for risk
and we ask for very little commitment.

We give each H.O.S.T. a New H.O.S.T. Home Kit that includes:

- welcome letter
- FAQ sheet with answers to many of the questions they might
have about leading a group
- DVD entitled "How to Start a Small Group," which covers the
following topics:
    be okay with inviting your friends
    be okay with who shows up
    be okay with not knowing all the answers

> be okay with taking the time to get to know each other
>
> be okay with not getting through all of the questions

- postcard-size invitations for inviting people to their group
- sample scripts to be used in visiting or phoning people to invite them to the group
- suggestions for how to invite people, what you will need for your first meeting, childcare options, as well as a campaign schedule

In addition to the kit, we also give the H.O.S.T.s access to eight online training sessions (each lasting less than ten minutes), which are available through our small group website, www.smallgroups.net/hosttraining.

### 2. Leader Training 1

Once leaders tell us they want to continue past the initial H.O.S.T. stage, we introduce them to our on-campus Leader Training 1. This is a basic training session for all of our new H.O.S.T.s or existing leaders who want a review. It is held several times per year and consists of one three-hour session. The course gives our new H.O.S.T.s a strategic overview of our small group ministry, explains a few basic survival techniques for hosting a group, and shares the support structure we have in place for them. It is taught by pastoral staff on the small group team, but it could be taught by a volunteer.

To start off the class, we provide them a large three-ring binder that will eventually hold all of their training materials. We then show a welcome video from Pastor Rick in which he congratulates them for taking the class, shares the importance of the role they play at Saddleback Church, and concludes with a prayer of blessing. Although the three hours are structured, there is time for questions and for the attendees to get to know the people around their table.

We also pass out two more resources:

1. Don't Lead Alone—a resource that explains the idea of purpose champions and instructs them how to develop purpose champions within their group.
2. 250 Big Ideas for Purpose Driven Small Groups—a resource that helps small groups achieve balance by giving them ideas and projects they might accomplish under each of the biblical purposes. Both are available at the resource section at www .smallgroups.net.

At the end of the session, we ask for written feedback and give them the document with the small group leader guidelines and leader values described in the previous chapter. If they agree to those guidelines and values, they continue down the pathway.

In addition, we have an online version available. We started online training out of necessity in 2009. Our small groups are spread out over five different counties, so online training makes it easier to "attend" training. Interestingly, in less than a year, we had more students in our online training than in our on-campus training. This allows us to bring together a group of new H.O.S.T.s at an off-site location. They meet with an area leader (a pastor on the small group team), and via a technology called Tokbox, they watch a live video of the instructor and see the same PowerPoint charts we use in our classroom version of Leader Training 1. They use the same booklet and also can speak to the instructor and each of the other students through text chatting.

After they have completed Leader Training 1 and signed the document with the small group guidelines and leader values, the church sends the H.O.S.T.s a letter of congratulations and a certificate that marks their completion of this first step. Because relationships are a vital ingredient to the success of our small group leaders and we want them to know they will not be alone in their journey, the next important step is connecting each H.O.S.T. with a mentoring *community leader* (CL)—a seasoned member of our small group ministry who *gets it and lives it*. (In the next chapter we will discuss how to recruit and develop community leaders.) From that point on, each H.O.S.T.'s community leader starts playing a key role in his or her growth process. The CL walks with the H.O.S.T. through each remaining step of the leadership pathway.

### 3. Leader Training 2

The third step along the leadership pathway is Leader Training 2. This five-module training course is led by the H.O.S.T.'s community leader and is often held in the CL's home. It focuses on deepening the five purposes in the lives of the leaders and showing them how to balance the purposes within their groups. These five modules can take up to two years to complete. We don't want H.O.S.T.s to take the next module until they are actually putting the previous one into practice. The five modules are:

1. Character—deepening your heart toward worship.
2. Skills—diving below the surface to understand true community.
3. Health—developing discipleship and helping your group and individual group members to be balanced.
4. Empower—helping you do ministry inside your group or with other groups, believer to believer.
5. P.E.A.C.E.—directing your group toward the P.E.A.C.E. Plan, which is our church's mission arm and is done personally, locally, and globally.

As H.O.S.T.s enter the Leader Training 2 phase, they start the discipleship module called Health. This addresses the imperative need for them to understand the value of balancing a group in the five biblical purposes. Once they have completed LT2 Health, they proceed down one of two paths. If they are leading a new group, they will focus first on the LT2 modules of Character and Skills, which complement the new journey they are on. If their group is more seasoned, we direct them toward LT2 Empower and P.E.A.C.E. These modules are a bit more challenging and designed for the small group with a strong foundation in place. Once H.O.S.T.s have completed Leader Training 2, they are official leaders.

### 4. Small Group H.O.S.T. Gatherings

The fourth step along the Leadership Pathway is our Gatherings. I wrote in chapter 7 of the importance of Gatherings and of showing your appreciation for your leaders. Our Gatherings show our leaders we care about them, and they also keep them tied to the vision. Remember, if you have multiple sites (one church in different locations), you can also use Gatherings as a way to unify the sites around the common vision.

### Four Important Relationships

Once you have your H.O.S.T.s in place, be sure they have the four relationships necessary to succeed:

1. *Relationship with Christ.* If a person does not have a relationship with Christ, nothing else matters—not leadership abilities, schooling, or personal charisma.
2. *Relationship with a mentor.* Whether you call him or her a coach, community leader, or mentor, every H.O.S.T. needs

someone to turn to for advice and guidance. More than one person may fulfill this role, but every leader needs at least one person who is coaching him or her.

3. *Relationship with a spiritual partner.* Every H.O.S.T. needs a spiritual partner of the same sex who provides accountability and support. The spiritual partner knows his or her struggles and next steps and holds the H.O.S.T. accountable. Unlike the mentor, who develops leadership skills, the spiritual partner is focused solely on spiritual development. This relationship is all too often overlooked.

4. *Relationship with an apprentice.* The H.O.S.T. should have someone in the group he or she is bringing along—a future H.O.S.T. Ideally, this person shares the responsibility of leading the group. A formal title is unnecessary, but the H.O.S.T. needs to intentionally develop another leader.

### Following Jesus's Example

When you are inspiring your leaders, you need look no further than the role model of Jesus the servant:

*Jesus fed his soul.* You cannot lead others unless you let God lead you. When your own heart is right with God, you can deal with the disappointments and the conflicts of ministry. Your leaders have to feed their souls, and it's important for you to nurture this mode of thinking. So often in the church when we recruit leaders, we give them the responsibility and then leave them on their own. There ought to be times when you gather your leaders in order to give them resources and tools to feed their own hearts and souls. There also ought to be times when *you* pull away from everyone and feed your own soul. "Very early in the morning, while it was still dark, Jesus got up, left the house and went off to a solitary place, where he prayed" (Mark 1:35).

> You cannot lead others unless you let God lead you.

*Jesus trained and discipled a few.* He gathered twelve men around him, and the biggest part of his ministry was investing in those twelve. In three years he took them from "follow me" to "die for me." He developed them and then entrusted them with the kingdom of God and the future of the world.

When he had finished washing their feet, he put on his clothes and returned to his place. "Do you understand what I have done for you?" he asked them. "You call me 'Teacher' and 'Lord,' and rightly so, for that is what I am. Now that I, your Lord and Teacher, have washed your feet, you also should wash one another's feet. I have set you an example that you should do as I have done for you." (John 13:12–15)

I love what Billy Graham said when asked, "If you were a pastor of a large church in a principal city, what would be your plan of action?" Mr. Graham replied: "I think one of the first things I would do would be to get a small group of eight or ten or twelve men around me that would meet for a few hours a week and pay the price. . . . Christ, I think, set the pattern. He spent most of his time with twelve men. He didn't spend it with a great crowd."[1] Who are you spending time with that will make a difference for eternity?

*Jesus ministered to the masses.* Jesus made himself available to minister wherever there was a need. "Jesus went throughout Galilee, teaching in their synagogues, preaching the good news of the kingdom, and healing every disease and sickness among people" (Matt. 4:23). You may not have masses following you, and you may not speak to the masses as Christ did. But when you are out and about, do the masses matter? Are people an interruption or an opportunity? Are you so task-oriented you miss the kingdom opportunities?

*Are people an interruption or an opportunity?*

## Money Talks

Although I wish money was never an issue, building a pathway requires a commitment of resources. Just like in your personal life, where a church spends its time and money is a reflection of what it values. If the small group ministry gets a very small slice of the pie when it comes to personnel and budget, this is a reflection of the perceived value of small groups. If you are going to build a healthy small group delivery system in your church, your budget will need to reflect this goal. It can start small, but use vision to show how it will help the church achieve health. See www.smallgroups.net/budget for examples.

## Questions

What type of training do you provide for your small group leaders?

_____

_____

_____

Do you have any type of continuing education for your small group leaders?

_____

_____

_____

How do you encourage current leaders to pass along training to new small group leaders?

_____

_____

_____

How is your training delivered?

_____

_____

_____

Do you have some type of leadership training pathway that is clearly laid out for your leaders from beginning to end?

_____

_____

_____

Do you have an intentional plan for feeding your leaders' souls as well as your own?

_____

_____

_____

# 14

# Laying the Foundation

## *Developing an Organizational Infrastructure That Works*

Care for the flock that God has entrusted to you. Watch over it willingly, not grudgingly—not for what you will get out of it, but because you are eager to serve God. Don't lord it over the people assigned to your care, but lead them by your own good example.

1 Peter 5:2–3 NLT

If you are not intentionally helping people get to God's destination, you're just in the way.

Ron Wilbur

In traditional small group ministry among churches of a thousand or more, there is usually a small group leader, a coach, and depending on the size of the church perhaps another level called a division leader, and finally, a pastor above that. At Saddleback we found the *coaching* piece of the puzzle was not working for us, so we flattened out our structure and reduced the number of levels by removing the coaching tier. Every H.O.S.T. (or small group leader) has a community leader (CL) above him or her. An area leader (AL) then oversees a number of community leaders. Typically, our community leaders work about ten hours per week and oversee twenty-five groups, and our area leaders work about fifty hours per week and oversee ten community leaders, or roughly 250 small groups.

Small Group Point Person  →  Oversees Area Leaders

Area Leader  →  Oversees Community Leaders

Community Leader  →  Oversees H.O.S.T.s

Due to our size, we need the added area leader layer. Most churches with under 300 small groups, however, will be fine with a small group point person and a group of community leaders. For more explanation about area leaders, go to www.smallgroups.net/arealeader.


## Span of Care

When I was at former churches, and even in the early years of my time at Saddleback, we used the typical coaching structure recommended in most small group books (a 1:5 ratio). I recruited coaches, and after about six months they would quit. Because recruiting comes easily to me, I simply recruited more people and kept filling the positions. But eventually, I couldn't keep up with the recruiting demand and had to look at what we were doing and why we were doing it. We looked over the feedback from exiting coaches and found the number one reason they had wanted to be a coach was to help people. We also found out their biggest frustration was that the people didn't want their help. Small group leaders would not return their calls. Some leaders had already been leading for over a decade and didn't feel they needed the coaching. Sound familiar?

As we looked at our groups, we started to see a pattern. We found the groups could be classified in one of four categories: (1) new groups, (2) seasoned groups, (3) veteran groups, and (4) stubborn groups. Looking at these categories, we realized all of the groups required some form of care, but not all groups required the same *type* or *amount* of care.

*Priority Care (new groups)*: These are our brand-new small groups. They are full of questions and unsure of themselves in the be-ginning, so we stay in close contact with them to give all of the support they need. They love the connection with community leaders.

*Personal Care (seasoned groups):* These are the early adopters who, when they like an idea, are ready to run with it. Typically these groups want time to interface with you in person. They are excited and ready for direction and encouragement. They are good enough to be dangerous! They have already completed Leader Training 1.

*Phone Care (veteran groups):* These are the groups that have been in the game and know what they are doing. Are they immune to issues? No. But when a problem comes up, they are veterans and know to whom they should go. These are the groups who want communication to be done primarily through phone and email. They are also typically mid-adopters. They have been meeting together for quite a while and have already completed Leader Training 2.

*Persistent Care (stubborn groups):* These are the late adopters—groups who have probably been doing small groups for many years. They may have been at the church before you, are slow to change, and are not hesitant to remind you of that fact. They are often reticent to try new things you suggest. The only thing they want to know is who to go to if they have an issue. Beyond that, they usually just want to be left alone.

For so long, small group theory has dictated that we need to give equal care to each group, but we have found that line of thinking is faulty—not every group needs equal care. Some groups are going to thrive with or without proactive care from a community leader, and persistent care groups are going to drain the life out of any community leader assigned to them. So we ask our community leaders to categorize their groups into one of the four categories above and proceed accordingly. We encourage them to spend 80 percent of their time with groups in the first two categories—priority care and personal care—so they are working with the people who want their assistance. This is *proactive care*, and we encourage them to stay on top of these leaders, work with them, and keep a close eye on them.

The other two categories—phone care and persistent care—should receive about 20 percent of the community leader's time. These two groups need *reactive care*, but they usually appreciate a prayer left on their voice mail once a month, a birthday card, or a note of appreciation sent by snail mail. The veteran groups just need to know you are out there and willing to help. The stubborn groups . . . well, what can I say? I could put a full-time pastor on one stubborn group and still not make progress. Bottom line, you don't have the resources to put into those groups, and neither do I. They love your church. They love Jesus. Change is just hard. Hang in there; they may come around in time, or they may not. Your role is to just love them.

### Community Leader Strategy

Our community leaders stay in contact with our H.O.S.T.s so they never feel they are doing small group ministry alone. The majority of a community leader's time should be spent giving care and building relationships with their groups in the four categories. We find Paul doing the same thing in Acts 18:11: "So Paul stayed there for the next year and a half, teaching the word of God" (NLT). After spending an extended time in Antioch building the leaders, he moved on and continued pouring into the lives of the new believers. "After spending some time in Antioch, Paul went back through Galatia and Phrygia, visiting and strengthening all the believers" (NLT). Building relationships and encouraging people is the most important aspect of the role of community leader. If CLs do not build solid relationships with their H.O.S.T.s, they will not have the foundation to lead.

**Figure 14.1**
**Community Leader Strategy 1:25**

**Community Leader Tasks**

Giving care and building relationships can include but is not limited to:

- *Working directly with the small group H.O.S.T.s and coaching them on the habits of a healthy group.* This includes issues such as shared ownership, subgrouping, being open to new members (whether they invite them into their group or they are open to the church placing them), meeting throughout the year, helping them see the value of formal and informal meeting times, and encouraging them to seek counsel for difficult problems. In addition, our CLs suggest ideas for balancing the purposes in the group. H.O.S.T.s are also taught how to use the Spiritual Health Assessment for every member of their group so they can develop a Spiritual Health Plan for the group as well as for each individual.
- *Working directly with the H.O.S.T.s and building a relationship based on accountability.* The community leader can encourage the H.O.S.T.s to take a personal Spiritual Health Assessment. Then the CL can help the H.O.S.T.s identify and take their spiritual next steps.
- *Praying for the H.O.S.T.s, their families, and each member of the group.*
- *Providing pastoral care for unhealthy groups or unhealthy group situations.* The CLs work with their area leader (the small group point person or staff pastor in smaller churches) to provide first-level counseling and biblical conflict resolution. This also includes coaching on how to deal with group members for whom extra grace is required. If a situation is out of control, the CL can assist in having it referred to the church leadership.
- *Providing pastoral care for life events such as baby dedications, baptisms, and hospitalizations as well as assisting at weddings and funerals.*

Giving care and building relationships should take the bulk of the CL's time, and what is left over will be needed for connecting people, training, and administration. This can include:

- Making reports and keeping records on the individual groups. Before you ask your H.O.S.T.s for a report, ask yourself this question: What am I going to do with the report? So often we spend a lot of time gathering information that doesn't matter. A big one is attendance. We really only need a census of who is in our groups a couple times a year. I am more concerned about the health of the H.O.S.T.s. If they are healthy, then I know they will be working on moving other people toward health. Leaders only have a certain amount of time to give. Do you want that time spent on reports or on health? Sometimes data and reports are necessary; just don't ask for more information than you are actually going to use.

- Helping interested people get connected with a small group and then ensuring that the H.O.S.T. follows up with the new person.
- Raising future leaders by working with the area leader to identify people in the small group community who have the potential to serve as community leaders.
- Helping the H.O.S.T.s understand the importance of training. This involves making sure new H.O.S.T.s complete Leader Training 1 on campus and then delivering the content of Leader Training 2 off campus through a personal relationship. (Typically the course is taught in the CL's home.)
- Serving as the access point for connecting people to others who can help them, such as professional counselors or financial counselors.

Former Dallas Cowboys coach Tom Landry, ranked as one of the greatest and most innovative coaches in NFL history, said, "Leadership is getting someone to do what they don't want to do, to achieve what they want to achieve." That is the job of the community leader—to get small group leaders to do what they don't want to do in order to achieve the goal of healthy and balanced groups. CLs are not there to merely be a buddy and develop a friendship with their small group leaders, though that does happen. Sometimes CLs have to push their leaders beyond their comfort zone and get them to do what they don't want to do, for the benefit of the kingdom.

As time goes by, two things should happen. First, the need for coaching a new group should decrease as they progress to phone care (see figure 14.2). Second, if the coaching is done relationally, the group should adopt the paradigm of your church strategy (see figure 14.3).

**Figure 14.2**

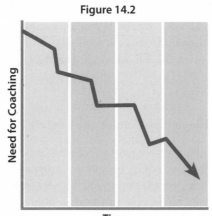

**Figure 14.3**

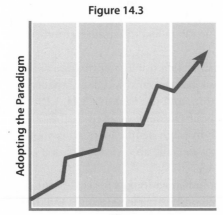

Getting people to do what they don't want to do is not an easy task. Small group leaders may have a misconception of the role of the CL, and they do not want someone from the church *checking up* on them. So one of the greatest challenges for any community leader is handling rejection. We teach our CLs to address this problem from the beginning. Instead of saying, "Hi. I've been assigned by the church to watch over you," the CL should say, "Hi. I'm your community leader, and I'm here to serve you. The church has asked me to help you in any way possible so that our group experience will be the best it can possibly be." When H.O.S.T.s complete Leader Training 1, we send them a letter thanking them for taking that step and introducing their community leader to them. If you are establishing new groups, this letter should come from your lead pastor. This helps start the relationship, so when the CL does call, the H.O.S.T. already knows his or her name.

### Recruiting and Developing Community Leaders

At Saddleback we use five steps to recruit and develop community leaders. They are enlist, equip, encourage, empower, and evaluate:

1. *Enlist*. There are people in your church who are ready and waiting for you to ask them to become involved in ministry. They probably won't come to you, but with some encouragement they will say yes. They have already been called by God, and he has already shaped them and prepared them since before they were born to serve in your ministry. It is your job to find them and give them the opportunity to fulfill God's plan.

We have a church database with information on all of our members. It tells us who has taken the various classes, what type of training they have participated in, and their unique S.H.A.P.E. When we started recruiting community leaders, we used that database to narrow the search and comb through people in small groups to find our prospects. By doing so, we came up with a list of over one hundred highly qualified prospects.

Once we had our list, we looked for two qualities: heart and availability. Did the person have leadership skills and the heart of a leader? Of equal importance, was he or she available? You can have the most gifted leader in the world, but if he or she does not have the time to serve, both of you will only end up frustrated. Don't overlook this important requirement.

After we narrowed down the list, we called each person on the list and personally invited him or her to come to a briefing at the church. We said, "We have this unique ministry opportunity, and we think you may be shaped for it. So we'd like you to come to a half-hour briefing to hear about it. Would you be willing to do that?"

About half of the people on the list agreed to come to the briefing. When they arrived, it was very casual. No PowerPoints. No sermons. No hard sell. We just sat down together and shared what God was doing through small groups at Saddleback and our vision for the role of community leader, explaining the importance of the role.

We then did something totally different—we didn't ask them to respond then and there. We weren't looking for people who were easily swayed and would accept an invitation into almost any ministry; we were looking for people God had called into small group ministry. So instead, we said, "We're not going to ask you to do this, because we're not sure you are the right person to do it. We want you to go home and pray about it, and if God puts it on your heart that this is the ministry he has called you to, then you let us know. We won't make a follow-up call. If you want to be involved in this ministry, you are going to have to call us."

After that, we still did not make it easy for them to become community leaders. When they called us and told us they were interested, we then asked them to fill out an application that included an area for them to tell the story of how they came to Christ. In addition, we asked them to sign our church's statement of belief and another statement stating they had no lifestyle issues that would be a stumbling block to others. After that, they each came in for a personal interview. If they passed the interview process, they then began their training as a community leader. That particular year, those who responded and went through that lengthy process were still serving over one year later.

2. *Equip.* Don't get caught up in too much formal training. If your community leaders have spent any time leading a small group, experiences from their own small group are the best training. Sometimes we can overthink and overtrain people. The most important skill for CLs is the ability to develop relationships. If they cannot develop relationships with their small group leaders, no amount of training will produce a competent community leader. When you think about equipping CLs, think relationally. Sometimes the best equipping you can provide is knowing them personally and making yourself available.

There is one area, however, in which we do encourage some formal training. At Saddleback, our community leaders are our *farm club.* They are the people who will most likely end up coming on staff. For this reason, after a year or so, we encourage CLs to get some type of seminary or Bible school training.

3. *Encourage.* Area leaders (or the small group point person in smaller churches) provide ongoing mentoring and encouragement for community leaders. They have monthly relational team meetings

with their CLs, which in many cases look just like small group meetings. They get together to eat, teach, sing, and pray. They compare stories, do case studies, review goals, and plan for upcoming events. In addition, the ALs will have a personal meeting with each CL once a month to pray, mentor, review, and personally encourage him or her. We suggest the ALs ask their CLs: "What's working?" "What's broken?" and "What's next?"

Another great tool is the 4 P's—praise, problem, plan, prayer. What's a praise in your ministry? The praises give us encouragement for why we do ministry. What's the problem? This identifies training opportunities. What's your plan? Figure out how you can build health. How can I pray for you? The level of prayer requests will reflect the level to which you have built your relationships.

4. *Empower.* To create successful community leaders, you must release them, give them power and authority, and empower them to make decisions. We operate on a loose-tight approach. Some things we hold tightly—such as our vision, mission, and core values. But personal style is loose—our leaders' style is a reflection of who God made them to be, and we honor that. How the CLs walk with their people and whether they get together with their H.O.S.T.s at Starbucks for coffee or meet at a Lakers game is their individual style, and that's very loose. We empower them to do the ministry in their God-given style.

5. *Evaluate.* We evaluate regularly. You cannot assume the community leaders are doing everything you tell them to do. Life is messy, and day-to-day struggles can often distract even the most well-meaning CL. You cannot manage what you don't measure, and you cannot evaluate without measurements. Otherwise you are just basing the evaluation on your own opinion, and God's opinion (truth) is the only one that counts.

Each of our community leaders have been given a list of measurements that are the things and experiences through which they are guiding their H.O.S.T.s. So when area leaders evaluate their community leaders, the questions they ask follow along those same lines:

Have your H.O.S.T.s taken Leader Training 1?

Have the members of your small groups taken the Spiritual Health Assessment?

Have your H.O.S.T.s taken Leader Training 2 Health?

Do your groups have Group Health Plans?

## Questions

How many levels of leadership does your small group ministry have?

_____

_____

_____

What is your span of care?

_____

_____

_____

Are you engaged in equal care or strategic care? Take time to put your groups into the four categories described on pages 178–79 and write down your evaluation of the best way to care for each group leader.

_____

_____

_____

How do you determine how much and what type of care your small groups receive?

_____

_____

_____

How do you deal with persistent care or stubborn groups?

_____

_____

_____

Who supports and encourages your small group leaders?

_____

_____

_____

How do they provide that support and encouragement?

_____

_____

_____

_____

# What Does This Mean for Overall Church Strategy?

15

# Sunday School and/or Small Groups

## Understanding How Groups Fit
## into Your Church

We proclaim him, admonishing and teaching everyone with all wisdom, so that we may present everyone perfect in Christ.

Colossians 1:28

Tell me and I'll forget, show me and I may remember, involve me and I'll understand.

Anonymous

The debate over Sunday school versus small groups continues. Each side debates the merits of their system while pointing out the flaws in the other system. A common question is: "Does your church have Sunday school or small groups?" which is often a veiled way of asking, "Is your church a traditional one that is stuck in the rut of Sunday school?" As more and more churches replace Sunday school with small groups, the common notion is that Sunday school is a system that traditional churches cling to while more modern and progressive churches move toward small groups. The truth, however, is not that simple or clear-cut. Both systems have their advantages and disadvantages. More important than the *system* used is the desired result: spiritual growth and health. If the goal is to teach the Word of God and apply the Great Commission and great commandment, does it matter if your people meet in a church classroom or a living room?

Before you decide whether to use Sunday school or small groups as a delivery system, make sure you understand your goal: spiritual health. Once you know what type of attributes you want to see in a healthy follower of Christ, then you can develop a delivery system to align with that purpose. At Saddleback, we believe a healthy follower is someone who is balancing the Great Commission and the great commandment in his or her heart and life. We believe the best way for us to develop healthy followers is through small groups. That doesn't mean, however, that you cannot use Sunday school to produce healthy followers of Christ.

The first two churches I worked at (one as an intern and one as a staff member) had Sunday school classes rather than small groups. The next two churches I worked at combined Sunday school and small groups. My previous church and Saddleback Church are totally driven by small groups. At each church there were pros and cons to their delivery systems. Looking back, I realize the most important thing, regardless of the delivery system, is to know *why* you have small groups or Sunday school. Many churches have Sunday school or small groups simply because that is what they have always done. They have given little thought to their desired result and whether the particular system they are using is the most productive for achieving that desired result.

Let's look at the benefits of both systems:

### Benefits

| Small Groups | Sunday School |
| --- | --- |
| ✓ longer fellowship time is more conducive to building deeper relationships | ✓ convenient meeting time (before or after worship service) |
| ✓ environment of living room is conducive to relaxed atmosphere, and seekers are often more willing to come to a home than a church building | ✓ convenience of location |
| | ✓ childcare provided |
| | ✓ easier to manage the leaders |
| ✓ infinitely expandable | |
| ✓ good stewardship of resources | |

Let's look a little deeper into these benefits.

## Sunday School

1. *Convenience of time.* Your people are already at church and it's easy for them to stay for an extra time slot. Time is a precious commodity, and people are more likely to attend if they are already there.

2. *Convenience of location.* Members don't have to drive to another place on another night. Church and Sunday school are held at the same location and on the same day.

3. *Childcare is provided.* Childcare is always an issue in small groups with children. Here it isn't.

4. *Easy access to leaders.* It's easier to communicate face-to-face with the class leaders than with small group leaders because they are all in the same building at the same time. Small groups meet at various times and locations, which makes it more difficult not only to guide your small group leaders but also to develop personal relationships with them.

> *More important than the **system** used is the desired result: spiritual growth and health.*

## Small Groups

1. *No time constraints.* Small groups are not under the constraint of a time slot before or after the worship service, which allows more time for fellowship and building relationships. Sometimes the best meeting is the one after the formal meeting stops.

2. *Relaxed atmosphere.* The environment is more conducive to conversation. There's just something about sitting in the relaxed environment of somebody's living room with a cup of coffee in your hand that allows people the freedom to begin to open up about what's going on in their world. That just cannot be replicated in a Sunday school classroom. In addition, for people who do not attend church, it is easier to take the first step of coming to a friend's home for a meeting than to go to a large church building filled with strangers.

3. *Infinitely expandable.* You have the potential of a small group in every home of every member of your church. Beyond that, groups sometimes meet in coffeehouses, workplaces, restaurants, or parks. Space is not a problem.

4. *Good stewardship.* Using small groups is good stewardship because the church does not need to provide meeting space (buildings) or additional parking space. At Saddleback, we have thousands of square feet of space in people's living rooms that we didn't have to build or pay the mortgage or utility bills. Our people are already living there, and now they can also use the space for God and his kingdom.

### Why We Chose Small Groups

Saddleback has never had Sunday school. When the church first started, they did not even have a building to meet in, let alone one to hold Sunday school classes. Rick moved from location to location, hauling chairs and nursery equipment every week and then storing them in his garage between services. Sunday school was never an option. When we finally had a building many years later, small groups were already an established part of the culture. Saddleback has always been a place where we are willing to sacrifice what we have to get where we need to go. Small groups were part of the strategy because small groups worked.

The clear choice for us is small groups. Jesus led people relationally, and we believe small groups are the best way to do that in Southern California. You need a venue where people can honestly share their lives, work on their problems, and be real together. So we have chosen the living room over the classroom.

*Saddleback has always been a place where we are willing to sacrifice what we have to get where we need to go.*

We are often asked, "What does that mean for churches with Sunday school?" Well, it doesn't have to mean anything. Again, the destination is health, balancing the Great Commission and great commandment. If your delivery system can achieve that, I'm for it! Later in this chapter I share some ways to make your Sunday school healthier. I don't care what your groups of people are called; I care about what those gatherings produce: health.

I receive all kinds of questions about Sunday school and small groups. Here are a few of the most common:

*Are small groups replacing Sunday school?*
Small groups and Sunday school don't have to be opponents. They can work together if they are aligned in the goal of producing a

follower of Christ. It is true, however, that there is a general trend away from Sunday school and toward small groups. Here are a few reasons churches are making the switch:

1. Churches that have multiple services and also hold Sunday school during those services usually struggle to find enough parking space. When a person attends a worship service and a Sunday school class, a parking space is tied up for two service times. If parking spaces are limited, this can be a real problem because people won't come to church if they can't find a place to park.
2. The second reason comes down to sheer economics. Sunday school requires classrooms, so your Sunday school attendance will always be limited to the classroom space you can provide. You might come to a point where the money that is being spent on classrooms could be better spent elsewhere in the community or the church. Small groups meet in homes, so space is never a problem for the church.
3. People often cannot give you two to three hours in one shot. Time is often our most precious commodity. With more demands on our people's time, going to a Sunday school and church service at the same time often just won't work. It can be easier for people to attend a small group on a different day of the week rather than tie up their entire Sunday morning.

*Will starting a small group ministry weaken an existing Sunday school? If so, why? If not, why not?*

When people were debating whether baseball should be televised on the new invention called *television*, the naysayers were worried that if people watched baseball on television, they wouldn't come to the ballpark. As history proves, this thinking was faulty. The same applies to this question. Having both small groups and Sunday school classes gives you more opportunities to develop people and reduces the excuses for not doing one or the other.

*Can Sunday school and small groups coexist in the same church?*

You bet! Sunday school and small groups can coexist as long as they are aligned and not competing with each other. This same potential for competing can happen with affinities such as men's, women's, couples', and singles' ministries in your church. If they are not aligned with your delivery systems to create healthy followers of Christ, any program can deter the effectiveness of your church. So make sure your Sunday school and small group vision, mission, and strategy are working on the same process and not building walls between the two. I suggest that both ministries report to the same person.

*What about the time slots for Sunday night or Wednesday night services becoming times for small groups?*

This may be a good starting point because your culture may have developed these times for people to set aside for church. But one of the benefits of small groups is that *they* pick the day and time that serves group members best. When *you* pick the time and day, you limit one of the strengths of using small groups as a means to deliver health.

> *Sunday school and small groups can coexist as long as they are aligned and not competing with each other.*

*Isn't Sunday school lecture-based while small groups focus on discussion and application?*

Actually, without the right strategy, even small groups can be nothing but a lecture from the small group leader. You need both biblical truths *and* application. People need a chance to learn and interact with each other as they apply these truths to their lives. If you are just providing lecture-based content, you are in danger of merely repeating what happens on the weekend. With the Internet, lecture-based content is easy to come by. Most Christians know far more than they apply to their lives. Make sure you have a good balance in your strategy.

*If you are doing both Sunday school and small groups in your church, should church members be expected to attend both?*

Absolutely not! You want to take them deep, not wide. The reason they are attending either one is to develop community, which serves as the foundation for holistic discipleship. You should be more concerned that they are living out the Great Commission and great commandment in their lives than whether they are attending every event the church offers. It is not a sin if they are doing both, but a busy schedule can be counterproductive.

*Do Sunday school teachers make good small group leaders?*

Depending on how you define what you want to see in a follower of Christ, the primary function of both the Sunday school leader and the small group leader is to understand where each student or group member is in his or her spiritual walk and then encourage that person to take the next spiritual step. Whether that is happening in a small group or a Sunday school class, the leader needs to be thinking about how to move his or her people along their spiritual journey. Once the leader understands that, then his or her particular gift set can be used in either a Sunday school class or a small group. The goal is to teach and apply the five biblical purposes found in the Great Commission and great commandment. By doing this you sharpen the strengths of the class or group members and develop their weak areas.

## How do I make my Sunday school healthy?

There are some practical steps you can take to help your Sunday school class maximize its health once your church has decided what its goal is for a healthy follower of Christ. (For Saddleback it is a person who balances the Great Commission and great commandment in his or her heart through fellowship, discipleship, service, evangelism, and worship.)

1. *Strategically set up your room.* Instead of having chairs set up in rows, use round tables. Placing class members around tables forces them to make eye contact with each other and encourages conversation. If your church can't afford round tables, just set up your chairs in small circles or horseshoes (open end of the horseshoe to the front of the classroom).
2. *Build consistency at the table.* Once you set up your room with round tables (or chairs in small circles or horseshoes), encourage class members to sit in the same spot each week so they can become better acquainted with those sitting next to them. When a group of new people come into the class, encourage them to start a new table. People will not feel safe enough to dive beneath surface-level conversations if they are sitting with new people each week. This will only happen with consistent relationships, which take time to build.
3. *Understand ratios.* If your class is larger than ten, start thinking about who can help you build health into every individual. If one of your goals is to know the spiritual health of each person in your class and encourage him or her to take a spiritual next step, then realistically, you can't know and follow up on more

than ten individuals. Identify leaders at every table to help you
in this process.

4. *Set the table for evangelism.* If your tables or circles seat eight,
   don't fill the table with eight people. Seat five or six people at
   the table and ask them to think about who they can invite to fill
   in the extra seats. Also, once they are seated in smaller circles,
   attendance accountability is a natural by-product. If you are
   seated with six people, they will notice if you are not there.
   Small gatherings like this develop an organic accountability.

5. *Know your sheep and help your sheep know themselves.* Plan
   a time for everyone to take the Spiritual Health Assessment and
   develop a Personal Health Plan. When class members take the
   assessment, they will learn the biblical purpose that is their
   strength (fellowship, discipleship, ministry, evangelism, or worship) and will be able to identify in which area they need to
   grow.

6. *Build spiritual accountability.* Once people have identified areas
   in which they want to grow, have them pair up with someone
   who will help them by asking the question, "Did you accomplish
   what you set out to do?" This checkup should be done as a
   natural part of the relationship. The Sunday school teacher and
   the table leader don't need to know what everyone is working
   on, just that each of them has a person who is checking up on
   him or her.

7. *Develop ownership.* Ask those who are strong in a particular
   purpose to help your class in that area. If someone at the table
   is strong in the area of fellowship, he or she can keep track
   of birthdays and anniversaries at that table or help the entire
   class to plan a social event. If someone at a table is strong in
   discipleship, that person can encourage table members to take
   the Spiritual Health Assessment and develop a Personal Health
   Plan. As your class works on each area, those who are strong
   can help individuals who are weak to grow. If a person is weak
   in the area of evangelism, the entire class can do an evangelism
   project, which will help that person grow.

8. *Know your limits.* Realize what you can do in the class time and
   what needs to be done outside of class. Generally, in a Sunday
   school hour you can only do discipleship. You can attempt doing
   fellowship, and maybe you can periodically use a class hour to
   only worship. The key is that you can't do all the purposes in

one Sunday school hour and you shouldn't attempt to do so. Determine what you can accomplish during class time and have people at a table or a group of tables work together to do a purpose outside of class time. Release your people to develop themselves. If you try to contain all learning experiences within the classroom, you will limit creativity and suppress the Holy Spirit.

9. *Think transformation, not just information.* Sunday school originally started in England to teach literacy to children on Sunday because they worked in the factory Monday through Friday, sometimes through Saturday. Thus the name Sunday *school.* Over time, biblical teaching was added, and then even later the secular teachings were dropped as labor laws were created and enforced and free education became available for every child. If we understand the roots of Sunday school, it is easy to see why so much emphasis is placed on *teaching.* In the context of its origin, that made perfect sense. Now Sunday schools are moving toward a missing piece of discipleship or spiritual formation: application. It is important that we present the information in such a way that the students take the *teaching* of Sunday school with them and *apply* it to their lives outside the classroom.

10. *Don't underestimate the power of discussion.* When you allow people time to discuss, they can talk through the biblical teaching you have given them. Discussion helps people see where they are and where others are, and it allows them to learn from each other. When people talk through issues and develop plans through discussion, accountability starts to form among those who are discussing their plans (whether they know it or not). Your greatest challenge as a teacher is to give your class time to discuss and own the principles you have taught. I encourage a 60/40 format: 60 percent teaching and 40 percent discussion time to explore how to apply it.

*How can I add small groups to my Sunday school–only church?*

Whether you are transitioning away from Sunday school or simply adding small groups to supplement your Sunday school system, be prepared for resistance. Most people are resistant to change, and in the case of Sunday school and small groups, that resistance can be very strong. Unfortunately, in recent years the two systems have been pitted against each other, and church members often feel compelled to defend the current system while fighting against the introduction of the new system.

As is the case with any change, *communication* is the key. Use every avenue of communication and use them often. If you are adding small groups with the intention of keeping Sunday school, be sure to let your people know that small groups are just another option for spiritual health. If you are transitioning away from Sunday school, do so slowly—very slowly. If you quickly pull the plug on Sunday school with little or no transition time, you could lose a large percentage of your congregation. Instead of seeing the Sunday school advocates as *enemies* of your new small group system, recognize them as the faithful servants who have attended those Sunday school classes week after week, perhaps for years.

I suggest that you think of this transition time in three stages:

1. *Patience.* If you were going on a mission trip, you would want to know something about the culture of the people. While you may feel you know your church culture, when it comes to leading change, you will be shaking the very foundations of your church. It is imperative that you understand not only the current culture but also your church's history and any buried trigger points that may be stumbling blocks to progress.

   a. Talk to key opinion leaders. Talk to the ministry leaders, but also look for *unofficial* leaders such as spouses of pastors, deacons, and elders. Talk to the people who work in the office. Interview that administrative assistant or children's ministry volunteer who has been at the church for twenty years. Ask people in the church who they think are the key opinion leaders. Who has influence and a passion for the future of the church? Who are the strong Sunday school proponents? You will want them on your side. Write down all of these names and be especially aware of names that keep coming up. Then go to those people and listen, listen, listen.

   b. Survey small group leaders past and current (if any). Find out what worked, what didn't, what they wish had been done differently. Survey Sunday school leaders and ask them for their thoughts about small groups. What are their reservations? What has been their experience with small groups?

c. Honor the past, but progressively move into the future. Be sure to honor the people who developed Sunday school or small groups before you. They may not have done it the way you want to do it, but because of their hard work and sacrifice, you have the opportunity ahead of you. This process is biblical and helps you live in the land of grace. Also, *grandfather in* any existing small groups. At the same time, however, focus on the new people who are adopting your paradigm (early adopters) rather than those who are waiting to see if you are around next year (late adopters). Remember, if you have existing small groups who have survived for a while with little or no direction, they probably have a *maverick spirit* and will keep going with little or no encouragement. They may be loyal, but the only way you will win them over is through relationship.

2. *Prayer.* Begin praying for responsiveness from your church. Enlist a group of people to pray for your new ministry. Ask Sunday school leaders to pray for the small group ministry. Hold times of prayer and dedicate times for fasting. When you ask people to fast, you will find out who is dedicated to your ministry! As you are praying, ask God to answer these three questions:

*Who?* Who is responsive to your vision? Who is seeing and feeling your passion? Who agrees with your goals and direction for the small group ministry?

*When?* When should you implement the plan? Pastor Rick has told me time and time again, "Don't let problem solving interfere with decision making." If you insist on every problem being solved before you commit to the decision, faith in God is absent. If you want to do a God-size ministry, you won't need to have it all figured out. I like to think of the three Ls: Look, Learn, and Launch. *Look* to see who is with you. *Learn* all you can. *Launch* when God tells you—and not a second before or after.

*Get together with your team and dream!*

*What?* What do you want to do? Microsoft used to have a logo line that I loved. It was, "Where do you want to go today?" It asks a question that requires action. Some churches have no idea where they want to go in a sermon let alone in a week, month, or year. Make sure you have a *plan* for adding small groups; don't just add them to your church because it seems to be the trendy thing to do. Groups must be seen as a way to either supplement or replace your Sunday school system. Be honest about this up front and don't ask your people to give time to something that is not strategic and intentional. Know what you want to do and where you want to go.

3. *Planning.* Failing to plan is the same as planning to fail. If you are going to add small groups to your church, you need to plan the action steps to take during each stage. The planning stage involves three components:

   a. First is the dream component. Without a dream, nothing will happen. Every great Christian leader had a dream—a vision of what that leader *knew* God wanted him or her to do. What is your dream? What are you seeking God to do? People don't give their time to merely fill their schedule, they give their time to follow a vision about which they are passionate. Get together with your team and dream!

   b. Recognize the obstacles and barriers ahead of you. Brainstorm with your team to determine what those might be before they happen. Also, get together to come up with answers to the questions church members are going to ask. This is a great opportunity to get all your team on the same page. Don't become discouraged when you hit an obstacle. Recognize it as a moment for God to work.

   c. Finally, set the plan in motion. This is the action component. Once you commit to a measurable goal with a deadline, things begin to happen. This is also a great time to enlist new people to become involved in your dream. Let them be part of the process. This will give them ownership and give you sanity.

## Questions

If your church has a Sunday school ministry, what are its strengths?

_____

_____

_____

What areas of your Sunday school could be improved upon?

_____

_____

_____

How might you make those improvements?

_____

_____

_____

If you have Sunday school, what is its purpose?

_____

_____

_____

Who are the most influential people in your church?

_____

_____

_____

How might you begin building relationships with these influential people?

_____

_____

_____

How might you be more intentional in praying for your ministry?

_____

_____

_____

# 16

## Making the Most of Every Opportunity

*How to Increase Connection*

Your love for one another will prove to the world that you are my disciples.

John 13:35 NLT

A healthy community is built on friendship, on people who are committed to the art of caring engagement, an art that only the gospel makes possible in its richest form.

Larry Crabb

While at small group conferences, I often hear something along the lines of: "We have about 30 percent of our church connected in small groups. Is that good?" The percentage varies; it may be 50 percent or even as much as 70 percent, but the question is always the same: "Is that good?" There is no right answer to that question. But I can tell you, your church will only be as connected as you are dreaming, praying, and hoping for. If you are at 30 percent small group (or Sunday school) participation, dream of the day when you are at 35 percent. If you are at 50 percent participation, dream of the day when you are at 60 percent. You are limited only by your ability to dream and your willingness to make that dream a reality.

When I came on staff in March of 1998, we were dreaming of the day when we would have more people attending small groups than were attending the weekend services. Through the grace of God and a lot of hard work and preparation on the part of the small group team, that dream has come true. Since 2004 we have had more people attending small groups than we have in our average adult weekend attendance. We don't see this as a threat to our church but as an indication of health.

## Importance of Connection

In Genesis we find Adam in the most perfect environment known to humankind: the Garden of Eden. Still, God uttered the words, "It is not good for the man to be alone" (Gen. 2:18). If Adam needed community in Paradise, how much more important is it to connect with people in our broken and sinful world? If you want people to become connected, you have to be willing to take on that responsibility and strategically plan to make it happen.

If you have ever bought a house, you probably worked with a Realtor. When you started looking at houses, the odds are you didn't buy the first one you saw. When you didn't buy the first one, your Realtor did not respond, "Aw, man, that's a bummer because that's the only one we've got. I don't have anything else to show you."

No, that didn't happen because Realtors are tenacious. They will show you houses until Jesus returns if you will just stay in their car. They want to make sure you get connected and they get a commission. Can you imagine if we had that same mentality? Very often our churches are lackadaisical in this department. Their attitude is that if you get in a small group, that's great, but if you don't, that's okay too. You have to develop a different mind-set. You need to be tenacious like a Realtor. We are working for a commission too—the Great Commission. Your job is to ensure the people of your church get connected into a small group. Failure isn't an option.

## Focus on the Benefits of Group Life

The people of your church have plenty of reasons for *not* joining a small group, so it is important to focus on the benefits and answer their objections before they ask the question. Some of the benefits we describe to potential group members include:

1. You will feel more connected to the church, people, and God. One of the things we tell our people at Saddleback is that they are not going to feel they belong here until they get into a small group. Attending the church on the weekends is very different from doing life together with a group of friends. The Bible encourages us to love one another, encourage one another, and pray for one another. There are over fifty *one another* commands in Scripture for us to follow. That is quite difficult to do during a casual *hello* or *good-bye* before or after the weekend service.

2. You will spend more time in the Bible and better understand it. In a small group you will have the opportunity to go through small group studies and ask questions of other believers. In addition, as you share experiences and struggles, you will see the truths of the Bible come to life in each other's lives.

3. You will receive support from other believers. Small groups provide excellent support during times of crisis. Being in a small group ensures that you will not face stressful times on your own.

4. A small group is an excellent place to develop your S.H.A.P.E. Not only can you discover your S.H.A.P.E. during a small group study, but the group also provides you with an excellent testing ground to try out your giftedness. Sharing your gifts in a group setting is much easier than jumping into an unknown ministry experience. In addition, other small group members can help you recognize your giftedness, develop your gifts, and encourage you in finding ways to serve.

5. You will grow in spiritual maturity. God promises where two or more are gathered in his name, he is there. Meeting with others and making Christ the center of not only your studies but also your lives will inevitably result in spiritual growth and an attitude of surrender and sacrifice for the kingdom.

## Channels of Communication

When you start thinking about ways to connect people, be aggressive and think out of the box. Look for times and events that are natural gathering points. In addition, develop new and creative ways to invite people into groups. The following are some suggestions.

*Personal invitations.* Most people get connected through personal relationships with other people, so encourage your small group members to personally invite people in their sphere of influence. They don't necessarily have to invite people into *their* group, but they should invite people into *some* group.

*Use testimonies from people in small groups.* People often see the pastor as the salesman. He is trying to get them to buy something. A testimony from an actual small group member, however, provides the experience of a satisfied customer. Utilizing testimonies during the services allows people to *see* lives that have been changed through groups—not just *hear* about the possibility of change.

*Pulpit influence.* People begin to recognize the value of groups when it is shared from the pulpit. Utilize any opportunity you may have to capitalize on the weekend services to connect people. In addition, suggest ways your lead pastor can incorporate small group stories into the weekend sermons. Your lead pastor telling a story from his own small group is much more effective than him telling others that *they* should be in a small group.

*C.L.A.S.S. 101.* Newcomers to Saddleback can take one of two steps: (1) they can join a small group, or (2) they can go to C.L.A.S.S. 101 (our class explaining the principles of membership). We know if they go to C.L.A.S.S. 101, they will be pushed into a small group, and if they go to a small group first, they will be pushed toward C.L.A.S.S. 101. It's a simple loop. We don't share this strategy with our people up front. Either choice they make is a win. Some want to check out C.L.A.S.S. 101 first because it's a onetime commitment. Some want to connect with a community right away. But we know we will get them into a small group and C.L.A.S.S. 101 eventually. So be very clear about what first step you want your people to take and make certain there is a link to small groups in that step.

*Other classes and events.* Events are a great opportunity for people to connect with those who are like-minded; help them continue the connection. For example, if you are offering a couples' retreat, encourage participants to join a couples' small group. Make every class and event an opportunity for people to connect.

*Bulletins, websites, Facebook, and Twitter.* Utilize your church's means of communicating with the congregation to raise awareness and create opportunities to connect. Most importantly, always give them information or a link so they can connect directly. Traditional marketing tells us people need to see something nine times before their awareness causes an action step. Once church members indicate they want to be connected into a group, it is vital that you respond quickly because that shows you care.

*Traditional marketing tells us people need to see something nine times before their awareness causes an action step.*

*Small group table visible at every weekend service.* At Saddleback, when you walk out to the patio, you will always see a table where people can get connected into a small group. Sometimes simple awareness is what it takes to connect people. Provide a place where people can ask questions on the weekend. This step is a constant reminder to join a small group.

*Target specific communities.* Over the next few years, over 9,000 homes will be built within a few miles of Saddleback Church. Those homes are on our radar; we are going after those communities. Get to know your community and where new communities are being developed. Be proactive.

*Start groups by affinity.* Set up various types of groups for people to join. Don't get stuck in the rut of only thinking about couples' groups. Other groups could include women only or men only, singles, college age, geographic areas, or focus on various ethnic groups who want to speak their mother tongue. For instance, if you have several Spanish-speaking people in your church, why not offer a Spanish-speaking group? At Saddleback we have over two hundred language-based groups such as Spanish, French, Chinese, and so on.

*View transitions as strategic times to help connect people.* We have learned it is often easier to connect people during events that mark some type of life transition.

> *Significant events*—Baptisms, baby dedications, weddings, or the birth of a child can cause people to become more aware of their need for spiritual guidance and growth.
>
> *Struggles*—Spiritual connectedness is vital when a person is dealing with the loss of a loved one, financial trouble, separation or divorce, blending a family, single parenthood, or health problems. One of the biggest struggles facing us right now is our young people being sent off to war, so we started offering groups for our people serving overseas. Military men and women are excited about getting to know Jesus in the battle zone.

*Spiritual steps*—It is important to draw into small groups those who are seekers, new believers, and people who are coming back to the church after a long absence.

*Seasonal beginnings*—The obvious options are fall, winter, spring, or summer. Also, the beginning of a new school year is a particularly good time for people to join groups. Think like Hallmark; they have come up with a card for every occasion, so think of occasions and seasons to start new groups. For example, in January people can start the New Year off right by getting into a small group. In February you can start couples' groups around Valentine's Day. The week after Easter can be spiritually significant to start new groups. In March start procrastination groups for those who didn't do it in January. You get the idea. People need a reason to join; give it to them.

*Starts and stops*—People can be encouraged to join a small group when a new curriculum series is introduced, when a new class starts up, or during a churchwide fall campaign. Provide opportunities that give specific starting and stopping times for those who are afraid to make a long-term commitment. God uses both change and pain to make people receptive to the gospel and to connect with others.

*Use connection events as a strategy to get people into groups.* When Brett Eastman joined our staff in July of 1997, he came up with a strategy we call a connection event. It was born out of sheer necessity due to a lack of leaders, and the idea has been refined over the years. As the strategy evolved and we updated the questions we ask, it proved to be a successful way to connect people quickly. You might want to give it a try in your church. We used our connection strategy as a primary way to draw people into groups until we came up with the campaign strategy in 2002. Now we use campaigns as our primary strategy and connection events as a secondary means of connecting people into a group.

We hold the connection event on campus, targeting the people who attend the church but are not yet connected to a small group. We recruit them through a variety of ways, including pulpit announcements, email invitations, flyers, videos, and personal invitations. It lasts about two and a half hours, and all you need is a room set up with some round tables. Depending on the size of your church, you might want to mark the tables for singles, couples, men only, or women only. Or you might want to divide the room according to geographic location. Once people arrive and are all seated at the tables, you pass out pieces of paper with discussion questions that focus on affinity, group experience, and their spiritual journey.

What is your name?

Where do you live?

What are some of your hobbies or interests?

Briefly (about two minutes) tell us about your spiritual journey to this point.

How did you start attending this church, and what do you like best about it?

What is your previous small group experience?

What is one thing you hope to gain by being in a small group?

What is one fear you have about joining a small group?

We allow them to get to know each other and discuss these questions for about an hour. Then after that discussion session, we guide them through the process of choosing a leader by giving them another series of questions:

Who is the most likely H.O.S.T. in the group?

Who has spiritual maturity and a growing heart for God?

Who has the most small group or ministry experience?

Who is someone you would be willing to follow for six weeks?

We then ask them to close their eyes and at the count of three, point to the person they feel would make the best leader. When they are all pointing, we instruct them to open their eyes and see who has the majority of people pointing to him or her. Then, and this is the critical part, we ask them to go around the table and tell why they selected the person they pointed to. Then we ask the person if he or she is willing to lead the group with a DVD curriculum for six weeks. (We start each of our new groups on the 40 Days of Purpose curriculum.) In the twelve years I have been at Saddleback, we have never had a person who went through this process say no to leading the group for six weeks. After the connection event, we provide H.O.S.T. training, curriculum, and a community leader to guide our new H.O.S.T.s along their journey.

If you already have leaders and are looking for people to fill their groups, you can begin the event by asking your leaders to each sit at an empty table. Again, if your church is large, you might want to have leaders for certain types of groups (women, singles, etc.), but the idea is for people to go to a table, bond with that leader and each other, and leave as a group.

The primary benefits of using a connection event to start groups are:

- Group members feel more of a sense of ownership after choosing a leader.
- New H.O.S.T.s are much more open to coaching and training.
- It is a very quick way to start multiple groups.
- Curriculum and training resources can be handed out immediately.
- If community leaders are in attendance, a relationship can be established right from the start.

For instructions on starting a connection event, see www.smallgroups .net/connection.

### Brainstorming Creates Ownership

If you are starting a small group ministry, or if you are considering retooling your existing small group ministry, looking for avenues of connection is an excellent way to start. Meet with your team and brainstorm all of the possibilities. Encourage team members to think out of the box. As they come up with suggestions and are part of the process, they will *own* these suggestions and be willing to employ them to connect people.

### Multi-Site Issues

*The relational connection to your sites is far more important than the reporting structure.*

For those of you overseeing multiple sites, remember that each site is at a different place of development as far as connection is concerned so different strategies are necessary for different sites. At Saddleback, the small group person at each site reports directly to their campus pastor, so they only indirectly report to me. This works for us because the relational connection to your sites is far more important than the reporting structure. But continue to brainstorm with this team just like you would with your direct campus groups.

## Questions

How many people do you want connected into small groups?

_____

_____

_____

Do the people of your church know the benefits of belonging to a small group?

_____

_____

_____

How do you promote these benefits?

_____

_____

_____

What avenues do you use to connect people into groups?

_____

_____

_____

How might you start using other avenues for connection? Who could help you use these new avenues?

_____

_____

_____

# 17

## Exponential Power

*Unleashing the Force of the Campaign Strategy*

> And the word of God increased; and the number of the disciples multiplied in Jerusalem greatly; and a great company of the priests were obedient to the faith.
>
> Acts 6:7 KJV

> In the last twenty-seven years at Saddleback, nothing—I mean nothing—has produced spiritual growth in our people deeper and faster than campaigns.
>
> Rick Warren

Saddleback Church was the first church to successfully use the campaign strategy, and beginning in 2002 we have developed campaigns such as 40 Days of Purpose, 40 Days of Community, and 40 Days of Love. A campaign is an intensive, churchwide focus on a particular aspect of spiritual growth that involves every age group. Weekend sermons, small group curriculum, children's Sunday school activities, student ministry programming, memory verses, newsletters, bulletin inserts, and websites are all used to get everyone on the same page for the duration of the campaign, which is usually about six weeks. Over

30,000 churches have successfully used Saddleback campaigns, and the strategy has proven to be an amazing vehicle for spiritual growth and connecting people into groups.

Before developing the campaign strategy, we used connection events to draw people into groups for churchwide events. One day we were in a management team meeting and Rick asked us, "How many groups do we usually start through connection events?" We answered, "About 300." He said, "That's great. Add a zero to that. Let's start 3,000 groups." We all knew that using connection events would never get us those kinds of numbers, and we told him as much. His answer? "Come up with a different strategy." And so we did.

*"If our church has ministered to you, would you in turn minister to your community?"*

This is when we came up with the H.O.S.T. strategy, and it became a huge piece of the puzzle. Rick stood in front of the congregation and said, "If our church has ministered to you, would you in turn minister to your community and be willing to H.O.S.T. a small group? You don't have to be married to them; just try it out for six weeks and see." We had so many people respond during the first service, we thought they had misunderstood. Rick repeated the invitation during the second service, clarifying that he was asking people to H.O.S.T., meaning: Have a heart for people, Open their home to a group, Serve a snack, and Turn on a video. We received an even larger response! During that first weekend, a total of more than 2,000 people volunteered to be a H.O.S.T. Now our only problem was to figure out how to prepare 2,000 people to fill and lead a group.

### Resources and Support

We started by thinking in simple terms. If someone had never led a group before, what questions might he or she have? Once we had a list of questions, we came up with an FAQ list to provide answers for our new leaders. You can see it at www.smallgroups.net/hosttraining. You can do the same for your new leaders. Make your FAQ list available online through your website, as a handout given to your new leaders on day one, as part of your ongoing training, or ideally all three.

Give them answers to something as simple as, "How do I invite somebody to my group?" During our first 40 Days of Purpose

Campaign, we gave our H.O.S.T.s a script they could memorize for inviting their friends and neighbors into their small group. That might seem like overkill, but you would be surprised how fearful some of your people will be about just talking to a neighbor. So we gave them a short, one-paragraph script.

We also included suggestions about how to plan for the first meeting, how to set up the room, when to offer the snacks, and what to do about name tags. Finally, we included information on how to use the curriculum and how to share ownership of the group. We tried to think ahead of time of any questions the H.O.S.T.s might have and then gave the answers to them in writing so they could read them in the comfort of their home.

## Saddleback Campaigns

We have experienced amazing spiritual and numerical growth during campaigns. For example, through a 40 Days of Purpose Campaign (in just 40 days):

671 new believers came to Christ and were baptized

1,200 new members took C.L.A.S.S. 101 and joined the church

worship attendance increased by 2,000

2,200 more people started serving in ministry

3,700 people committed to a world mission project

There are particular distinctions of a Saddleback campaign, including:

- Small groups provide tremendous potential for exponential growth.
- We use the term *H.O.S.T.* instead of *leader* to lower the bar and increase participation.
- The H.O.S.T.s are responsible to fill their groups with people they already have a relationship with, increasing the likelihood that the group will continue after the initial study.
- Senior pastor buy-in is obvious through his involvement from the pulpit, thus increasing the perceived value of small groups and community.

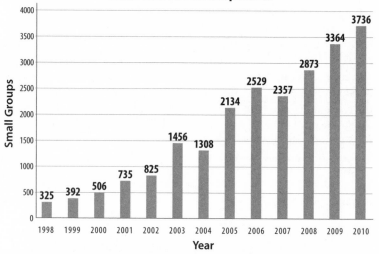

**Figure 17.1**
**What God Has Accomplished**

- Short-term commitments (usually six weeks) are easier to obtain.
- DVD-based curriculum is easy to use and takes the pressure off the H.O.S.T.
- Campaign topics have a wide appeal, so more people are likely to want to participate.
- Small groups are the distribution point for materials of the campaign, so the people of the church feel as though they are missing out on something if they do not join a small group. If people want the book, the key tags, or whatever promotional material you are using, they have to join a small group to receive it.
- H.O.S.T.s have the support of a community leader who encourages, answers questions, gives guidance, and prays for them.

### Think Long Term

As your church does campaigns, you will start and lose a lot of groups, but if you retain a portion of the groups started, you will be ahead of where you started. See figure 17.1 to see how this has played out at Saddleback.

In our first 40 Days of Purpose Campaign, we started 2,154 new groups. By February of the following year, we still had 1,456 of those 2,154 groups. Now, you can view that one of two ways: (1) we lost about 700 groups, or (2) we gained almost 700 groups.

Table 17.1

**Small Group Campaign Growth and Retention**

| Campaigns | July 1 Groups | October 1 Groups | February 1 Groups |
|---|---|---|---|
| 40 Days of Purpose 2002–2003 | 825 | 2,154 | 1,456 |
| 40 Days of Community 2004–2005 | 1,308 | 2,545 | 2,134 |
| 40 Days of P.E.A.C.E. 2005–2006 | 2,045 | 3,041 | 2,529 |
| 40 Days of Purpose (2) 2007–2008 | 1,948 | 3,501 | 2,873 |
| 40 Days of Love 2008–2009 | 2,529 | 4,125 | 3,364 |
| Life's Healing Choices 2009–2010 | 3,486 | 4,469 | 3,736 |

When we looked at the reasons why people did not continue with their group, we found it was not because they did not have a good experience. It was more likely that life got in the way or that we didn't have the infrastructure in place to support them. Two years later, with our infrastructure in place, we did our 40 Days of Community Campaign and our retention rate went from 68 percent to 86 percent. We learned by stepping out in faith and attempting the seemingly impossible, by moving ahead before we had all of the details worked out, and by making mistakes and learning from them.

Anyone can now benefit from our experience by purchasing one of our Saddleback Church Campaign Kits (www.saddlebackresources .com), which come with full instructions on how to run the campaign from start to finish. The instructions explain what type of teams you need to develop, and the kit provides a calendar timeline and training

DVDs for you and your team to watch. Having lived through nine campaigns in my twelve years as small group pastor at Saddleback Church, I have discovered a strategy is only as good as the foundation and follow through. As they say, the devil is in the details.

A churchwide campaign is an exponentially positive or negative experience for a church depending on how you approach it. Based on my experience and a few battle scars, I have developed the following twelve tips to ensure a positive outcome.

*A strategy is only as good as the foundation and follow through.*

1. *Know the compelling question.* When you do a campaign, you need to know the question the campaign will answer. For example, in our 40 Days of Purpose Campaign, the question was, "What on earth am I here for?" The compelling question gives your people a reason to join a small group and attend the corresponding weekend services. It provides your small group leaders with motivation to invite others into their small group. Without a compelling question, the congregation won't understand the central theme or the reason for the campaign.

2. *Align children, student, and adult ministries.* A lot of churches that do a campaign miss the alignment by only doing it for the adults. When your children and teens memorize the same Scriptures, read similar themes, do projects together, and listen to the same weekend message, everyone is on the same page. Discussions naturally flow into the home from parent to child and child to parent. Without churchwide alignment, you are unintentionally sending the message that only the adults of the church are important. Don't make that mistake.

3. *Stick to the principles and apply your own methodologies.* When aligning your campaign for children and students, adapt the material to their learning level. So if the adults are memorizing a Scripture, the children may learn part of the same Scripture instead of the whole Scripture, because that is appropriate for their level. The same principle should be applied to your entire church. Weekend messages need to be adapted to your church context and culture. Small group questions can be adapted to the needs of the group. If there is a churchwide or small group project, it should stay true to your church culture. For example, if your church has a strong presence in the homeless community, serve those same people with your campaign projects.

4. *Language matters.* One of the most significant things we learned through recruiting for our campaign was that language matters!

Campaign material is delivered through small groups, so it is vital that you have plenty of people ready to *lead* a small group. It didn't work well when we asked for lay pastors because the people didn't feel they were pastors. We then changed the term to *shepherd leaders*, which failed because they didn't connect with the term *shepherd*. Next we tried *small group leader*, but nobody wanted to be the leader due to perceived inadequacies or lack of time. Then we asked for *H.O.S.T.s*, and all of a sudden we had plenty of volunteers! Interestingly enough, we never changed the duties of a small group leader, just the language. That was enough. All of the preconceived notions of what it takes to be a *leader* just fell away. If a H.O.S.T. continues with the group after the campaign, we enter them into our Small Group Leadership Development Pathway (see chapter 13), which provides them with the relationships and resources to nurture and build their leadership skills.

5. *Employ various avenues of learning.* The campaign strategy uses a common theme that is taught in various ways to help people learn through their particular learning style. People can learn through listening to the weekend services. People can learn through discussing topics in their small groups. People can learn through doing hands-on projects with their small groups. People can learn through memorizing Scripture. And people can learn through reading as they work through the campaign materials in their small groups.

6. *Once a year is enough.* When you do too many campaigns in a year, two things happen: your volunteers who pulled it off won't be able to manage doing another campaign so soon, and your congregation won't experience the anticipation of an upcoming event. At Saddleback we do one campaign a year, and trust me, it comes around again quickly!

7. *Provide a clear start and end date.* Our campaigns last forty days, which includes six preaching weekends focused on the campaign topic and a forty-day devotional reading, with a couple days of grace! This is a short enough commitment that most people are willing to try it but long enough to instill good habits. When you have a clear start and end date, people are more willing to come along for the ride.

8. *Expect high intensity for staff, volunteers, and members.* One of the secrets of a successful campaign is sustaining high intensity for forty days and then backing off to allow staff and volunteers time to recover and give members time to process the experience. Let your church calendar return to normal and give your small groups time to stabilize. For a campaign to happen successfully, you must clear

the calendar for the duration of that campaign. Stop programs and events that could be distracting—sometimes *good* programs can stop *great* things from happening in a campaign. So once the campaign concludes, allow the calendar to get back to normal. Also, a campaign creates many new groups, and when the campaign ends, you need time to assess where those groups are. Some will continue and some will stop, but without the margin and infrastructure to check in on these groups, you will start a lot of groups and lose the same amount.

*You don't have to be an expert; you just have to be one step ahead of that new small group leader.*

9. *Remember and celebrate!* Too often the church does a great job of recruiting and getting the job done but then fails to appropriately celebrate a job well done. After the campaign, be sure to hold a celebration and express your gratitude for all of the hard work done by staff and volunteers. Take time to remember and celebrate God's work. Share stories of success and gratitude. When you don't take the time to celebrate, you are increasing the possibility of burnout in your staff and volunteers. In the Bible we read of many instances when God had people stop and remember the miracles he did. Why? Because he knew people forget. When you celebrate, you etch God's work on your people's hearts. Often we give little reminders such as key chains so that when people see them, they will be reminded of how God worked through so many people's lives and then celebrate the campaign into which they put so much time and energy.

10. *Plan for after the campaign.* It is important to have an infrastructure in place to support your new groups. You don't have to be an expert; you just have to be one step ahead of that new small group leader. At Saddleback our infrastructure includes community leaders who oversee new small groups and the Small Group Leadership Development Pathway to train small group H.O.S.T.s who choose to continue to lead.

Give your groups a next step. Around the fourth week of the six-week campaign, we encourage groups to determine what their next step will be. Will they continue or part ways? We provide curriculum suggestions and encourage them to get the new material as soon as possible. Very often, just avoiding downtime can make the difference in whether or not a group continues.

11. *Give people an out after the campaign is finished.* In a campaign it is important to give people permission to leave their group or

disband the group altogether. I know this feels counterintuitive, but it will serve you well. Now, let me be clear, I want them to continue, and I want to give them every possible reason to stay together; but on the other hand, I don't want them to feel guilty if their group doesn't continue. Why? Because when they do what you have asked, they need to be rewarded and thanked, not be criticized for not continuing. I have learned that when you give people permission to stop meeting at the end of the campaign, they will be there for the next campaign. And during the next campaign, they just might stay with their group.

12. *Budget to remove financial obstacles.* When we do a campaign, we pay for everything. In order to make a spiritual impact on anyone who joins a small group, we provide the devotional reading books, memory key tags, prayer guides, small group DVDs, and small group study guides. It's a lot of money up front, but it brings huge dividends on the back side. By investing in your church in this way, it shows your people not only that you care about them but also that you are willing to put your money where your heart is.

> *Sometimes good programs can stop great things from happening in a campaign.*

As you dive into a campaign, take the time to learn from other churches in your area that have done a campaign. Their experience will save you a tremendous amount of time and energy. You can find other churches through the Small Group Network (www.smallgroupnetwork.com).

## Questions

Have you ever done a campaign?

_____

_____

_____

If so, what were the benefits?

_____

_____

_____

What could you have done to improve upon the experience? How will you improve future campaigns?    .

_____

_____

_____

If you haven't done a campaign, what are you waiting for?

_____

_____

_____

# Do I Have
# What It
# Takes?

# 18

# Things I Wish Someone Had Told Me

## *Lessons from My Journey*

Each one should test his own actions. Then he can take pride in himself, without comparing himself to somebody else, for each one should carry his own load.

Galatians 6:4–5

Leadership is not so much about technique and methods as it is about opening the heart. Leadership is about inspiration—of oneself and others. Great leadership is about human experiences, not processes. Leadership is not a formula or a program, it is a human activity that comes from the heart and considers the hearts of others. It is an attitude, not a routine. More than anything else today, followers believe they are part of a system, a process that lacks heart. If there is one thing a leader can do to connect with followers at a human, or better still a spiritual level, it is to become engaged with them fully, to share experience and emotions, and to set aside the processes of leadership we have learned by rote.

Lance Secretan, leadership expert[1]

Jim Tressel, head football coach for the Ohio State Buckeyes, gives a great insight into being a coach:

My job as a coach is to do more than just teach the Xs and Os of the gridiron. I recently heard someone explain how the word *coach* came to be applied to an athletic context. The etymology of the word, at least in part, comes from the old stagecoaches that were used to transport mail, valuables and people before the advent of motorized transportation. Whether a coach was drawn by a horse or a steam locomotive, it carried or conveyed something or someone from one place to another. If you put yourself into a coach, you knew you would end up at your desired destination. In the same way, athletic coaches carry players or teams from one point in their development to the place they want to be.[2]

One of the things I regret is that at the start of my ministry, I didn't have someone who could speak into my life. Now, I'll admit that I could have asked someone to steer me or coach me, but you don't know what you don't know. All too often in ministry, as long as you don't screw up or have complaints coming into the church office, you are doing all right. As long as there are no complaints, there is no coaching. When coaching happens only because of mistakes, it becomes punitive rather than positive.

*When coaching happens only because of mistakes, it becomes punitive rather than positive.*

In small group ministry there are some things that are common sense, some that are learned along the way, and some that have been passed along from those who have gone before us. I don't want to assume anything, so follow with me as I share the things I learned the hard way and the things I wish I had known from day one of ministry.

### Remember, Everyone Poops

When someone new joins our small group team, I like to show him or her a little book Lisa and I used to read to our kids called *Everyone Poops*.[3] This might not be the typical book used for theological training, but I think it is a great place to start. New people coming on board often feel inferior to others already on staff and think they have nothing to contribute to the team. Since the ministry has an established format, they feel they must go along even though God may be leading them in a different direction.

I never want that to happen. So I use the book to remind my staff we are all sinners saved by grace and called by God—and we all poop. Just because I happen to lead the team, that doesn't mean I have all the right answers. But as the leader, I do have to make some hard decisions. Sometimes everyone likes them, and sometimes they don't.

Being a good leader requires knowing that every part of the body is important and that even if you don't agree with someone else's proposal, it may be the idea that starts the team on a new journey for better kingdom work. I use the term *leading up* to refer to team members seeing what could be done and telling their supervisor. We all need a reminder that *leading up* should not be suppressed but instead is our biblical duty.

## Listen and Learn

One of the worst things you can do is read a book on small group ministry or go home from a small group conference and immediately try to quickly implement all you have learned. Change requires time, especially in a church setting. Take time to evaluate as you learn and think about how you might slowly incorporate new ideas into your church culture. Get to know the people who will be affected by the change and look at it from their eyes. You still need to make changes, but you also need to make sure these people are heard. "Only simpletons believe everything they're told! The prudent carefully consider their steps. The wise are cautious and avoid danger; fools plunge ahead with reckless confidence" (Prov. 14:15–16 NLT).

> *Leading up should not be suppressed but instead is our biblical duty.*

## Check Your Motivation

Does your ministry come from your heart, or are you climbing the ministry ladder and merely checking off things on a to-do list? Are you motivated to serve God or your own ego? Do you feel a sense of compassion for the people you are serving, or are they interruptions in your daily routine? As a leader you must continually evaluate your heart, assess your compassion, and check your motives.

*Heart.* John 10:1–18 tells us the Good Shepherd will lay down his life for his sheep. You probably will never be asked to lay down your life, but if you want to fulfill the vision and mission of your small group ministry, there are two things you must lay down: your finances and

your time. Those are the two areas you will have to surrender. Every
person in ministry could be making a lot more money in traditional
fields of secular employment. But God has you where he wants you.
Be sure to remember that when you start looking
*Evaluate by*               at your friend's house or car or lifestyle.

*health, not*                        *Compassion.* Luke 19:41 tells us that "as [Jesus]
approached Jerusalem and saw the city, he wept
*numbers—period.*     over it." Your ministry must be carried out with
this same compassion. Luke describes Jesus look-
ing down on Jerusalem and seeing all of the lost people—sheep without a shepherd. This sight brought tears to his eyes; he had compassion
for the people he was serving. How do you see the people of your
church? Of your greater community? Of the world at large?

*Motivation.* "For we must all appear before the judgment seat of
Christ, that each one may receive what is due him for the things done
while in the body, whether good or bad" (2 Cor. 5:10). This verse tells
us that at the end of time there is going to be a judgment. We will
appear before Christ and take what's coming to us as a result of our
actions. God will require the answer to two questions: (1) Did you
accept my Son as Lord and Savior? (2) What did you do with what I
gave you? I am going to have to answer those questions, and so will
you. God knows our motivation. We need to take time periodically to
check our motivation and make sure our hearts are in the right place.
I can guarantee you that I am going to do everything I can to hear in
heaven, "Well done thou good and faithful servant."

## Don't Neglect Health

The number of groups in your church is *not* an indication of success.
Base your success on those you make healthy by focusing on supporting and not reporting for your groups. The health of the people
in those groups is an indication of success. Evaluate by health, not
numbers—period.

## Honor Your Forebears

Wherever your small group ministry, it is based on a foundation that
was built by someone else. Honor that foundation and those who
went before you. You may not agree with them and how they did

ministry, but their legacy (good or bad) gave you the opportunity that is now before you.

## Understand That You Are a Masterpiece

As a parent, you would never compare your child's value to that of another child. In the same way, never compare your small group ministry to other small group ministries. God gave you and your church a very specific purpose. Discover and act upon that purpose and don't waste time trying to imitate someone else or some other church.

Lisa and I were at Musée d'Orsay in Paris, France. Lisa loves impressionist art. Me? Well let's just say I missed that passion when God was wiring me. In our home we have a copy of Monet's *Jardin à Giverny*. At the Musée d'Orsay we saw the original, which was a dream come true for Lisa. But even I was taken aback by the painting; the colors took my breath away. I was unprepared for the sheer presence of this artwork.

*God gave you and your church a very specific purpose.*

Remember that you are God's original masterpiece, his artwork. People will be inspired by seeing God's work in you. Never settle for being a copy.

## Live Out a Faith Worth Imitating

We all need to ask ourselves: Do I have a faith that is worth imitating? Do they look at me and say, "I want to live that guy's spiritual life"? If it were possible for somebody to have your spiritual life for seventy-two hours, when the time was over, would that person want to give it back or hang on to it? Are you living the life you are calling others to live?

## Set Your Priorities and Keep Them

It is possible to do ministry in such a way and at such a pace that your work *for* God can destroy the work *of* God in you. You can get so caught up in the daily activities of ministry that there's nothing happening in your own life. It's like the guy who says, "I didn't have time to pray today because I was late for a prayer meeting." We can become so filled with activity that religious activity takes the place of spiritual intimacy. Your heart can begin to harden and you start to burn out. You find yourself becoming jealous of the spiritual intimacy other people experience. Or worse yet, you begin to lose your faith. You tell yourself that if you don't get all of this work done, then it won't get done. But the truth is, if you don't slow down and spend time with Jesus, nothing you do is going to matter.

Tithing teaches us God can do more through us with our 90 percent than we can do on our own with 100 percent. It is the same with our time. God instructs us to rest on the Sabbath. He can do more through us in six days than we can do on our own in seven. Tithing isn't about money and the Sabbath isn't about time; they are about trust and obedience. There will always be more ministry than we have time for, so you might as well do it God's way.

## Stay Humble

We all need to keep in mind that there is no job too low for us. There are things we do because of our gifting and things we do to serve the body. I remember when my daughter, Erika, was learning about spiritual gifts. It was a typical day at our house, and I asked her to take out the trash. She looked at me with determination and said, "Dad, that's not my spiritual gift"—which gave me a great teaching opportunity on John 13, after numerous other thoughts went through my brain! "Now that I, your Lord and Teacher, have washed your feet, you also should wash one another's feet. I have set you an example that you should do as I have done for you. I tell you the truth, no servant is greater than his master, nor is a messenger greater than the one who sent him. Now that you know these things, you will be blessed if you do them" (John 13:14–17). Erika learned that taking out the trash serves the family, even if it isn't her gifting, and from that day on she happily took out the trash without complaint. . . . Yeah, right!

## Continue Learning

Rick has a great saying: "all leaders are learners." Learning is as much an attitude as it is a cognitive function, and learning happens in many ways. How do you learn best? Books and conferences are one way to learn, listening to those around you and asking for their input into your life is another. Each year I email my staff and ask them for a review of the previous year; I call it my 360 Review. I ask them to do it anonymously, so they will feel free to speak the truth. The letters are sometimes painful to read, but they make our team better. Here is an example of a typical request for a 360 Review that I recently sent to them:

> I want to again get your feedback. To keep things anonymous, everyone use the same font: Arial 12 point. Please give me feedback on what would make our team better.
>
> 1. Write as much as you want on what you like about the team.
>
> 2. Write as much as you want on what would improve our team.
>
> 3. Write as much as you like on what resources you think our team needs.
>
> 4. What are the things I do in how I lead the team that you appreciate?
>
> 5. How could I improve in leading the team?
>
> 6. PRINT out your response, and do not include your name. Place it in an envelope, and put it on Deanna's chair. She will collect them and give them to me.
>
> 7. DEADLINE is Friday, May 29.
>
> You may be asking, "Do I have to do this exercise?" No, but the only way I can improve or the team can improve is through your responses to the questions above.
>
> "Do I need to answer all the questions?" No, but I sure do value your input.
>
> "Do I have to say nice things about Steve Gladen?" No. I learned long ago that 10 percent love what I do, 10 percent think they could do a better job leading, and 80 percent don't even know I lead the team. So help me improve. I view criticism as you wanting me to grow to be better. If that's not what's in your heart, we have a bigger issue!
>
> I appreciate each of you!

## Develop a Good Relationship with Your Lead Pastor

It is important to have a good relationship with your senior pastor. In reality, our lead pastors are our greatest small group advocates. They set the direction for the entire church and model desired behavior. If they don't have time to be in a small group, the chances are that your people will use the same excuse. Don't be discouraged, but use this as an indicator that you need to *lead up*. You may not have the positional authority to tell him what to do, but you can lead up relationally to share the values and benefits you see. Take the time to build a relationship through spending time together before you engage in an agenda.

*Our lead pastors are our greatest small group advocates.*

## In Closing

As I write these last few sentences, I pray that something in this book will help you to be more effective in serving our heavenly Father and building his kingdom. You may not do everything like Saddleback does. You may not like our methodology. That's okay! Your church may never do a campaign or use the H.O.S.T. strategy. But don't miss the opportunity to use some of the principles in this book to develop your own strategies. Encourage groups and your individual members to live out the Great Commission and the great commandment.

Please don't let the enemy paralyze you with fear or isolate you. Use this book, connect to the Small Group Network, www.small groupnetwork.com, or email me at steve@stevegladen.com. You matter to God, and building health in his church through small groups is an incredible privilege.

## Questions

Who's really in charge? Are you taking instruction and leading from your heavenly Father, or do you have your own agenda?

_____

_____

_____

How do you measure your self-worth? Is it by the things you do, the things you have, or the people you influence? Are your standards of worth the same as those of God?

_____

_____

_____

What kind of leader are you? Are you willing to embrace your role as leader and make the necessary changes to keep improving on your leadership style?

_____

_____

_____

What is most important to you? Are your priorities in keeping with the way you spend your time?

_____

_____

_____

What will you do with your life? You have a limited amount of time on this earth; how will you spend your days?

_____

_____

_____

How far are you willing to go? Are you 100 percent committed to fulfilling God's purpose for your life? If so, what is one thing you can do today to continue on your path? If not, what will it take for you to reach a full commitment?

_____

_____

_____

How will you remember God's calling in your life? As a leader in ministry, you have been called by God. How will you honor that calling? What will you do when times get tough to ensure you stay on God's path?

_____

_____

_____

# Notes

## Chapter 2 The Saddleback Difference

1. Arthur F. Holmes, *All Truth Is God's Truth* (Grand Rapids: Eerdmans, 1977), 32–33.

2. Rick Warren, *The Purpose Driven Church* (Grand Rapids: Zondervan, 1995), 27.

3. Ibid., 36.

4. Ibid., 43.

5. Ibid., 146.

6. *Merriam-Webster's Collegiate Dictionary*, 11th ed., s.v. "balance."

7. Warren, *Purpose Driven Church*, 103.

## Chapter 4 Is Your Vision Blurry?

1. From televised press conference, November 17, 1973.

## Chapter 7 Don't Lead Alone

1. Dietrich Bonhoeffer, *Life Together: A Discussion of Christian Fellowship* (San Francisco: Harper, 1954), 94.

2. Max Lucado, *Cure for the Common Life: Living in Your Sweet Spot* (Nashville: W Publishing Group, 2005), 1.

3. Erik Rees, *S.H.A.P.E.* (Grand Rapids: Zondervan, 2006), 25–26.

## Chapter 13 The Road Ahead

1. Billy Graham, quoted in Robert E. Coleman, *The Master Plan of Evangelism* (Grand Rapids: Revell, 1997), 111.

## Chapter 18 Things I Wish Someone Had Told Me

1. Lance Secretan, "Leadership Building Quotes," Leadership Building, January 5, 2010, http://leadershipbuilding.com/tag/warren-bennis.

2. Jim Tressel, *The Winners Manual: For the Game of Life* (Carol Stream, IL: Tyndale, 2008), 19.

3. Taro Gomi, *Everyone Poops* (Brooklyn, NY: Kane/Miller, 1993).

**Steve Gladen** was born and raised in Columbus, Ohio. He attended Evangel University in Springfield, Missouri, where he earned a BA in biblical studies with minors in Greek and philosophy. From there he moved to Pasadena, California, and received a master's of divinity from Fuller Theological Seminary, with a concentration in pastoral counseling.

While completing his master's, Steve was awarded an internship at a local church in the San Fernando Valley, which started his full-time pastoral career in 1982. Influenced by the small group model taught at Fuller, Steve began to realize the value of small groups in connecting people to the church and in the discipleship process. Throughout his ministry and in churches of varying denominations and sizes, he has successfully implemented the small group strategy in youth ministry, singles' ministry, and overall church structures.

Steve joined the staff of Saddleback Church in February of 1998 as pastor of small groups. He oversees the strategic launch and development of the small group community. In 2006 he founded the Small Group Network, a network for leaders of small group ministry (www.smallgroupnetwork.com). Using the Great Commission and great commandment as inspiration, Steve encourages every group member to balance the five biblical purposes in their soul and groups.

Steve does consulting and seminars throughout the United States and internationally, championing small groups and teaching what it means to have small groups with purpose. Steve and his wife, Lisa, reside in Southern California, have been married since 1989, and have two children, Erika and Ethan.

# SADDLEBACK CHURCH
## Equipping the next generation of small group leaders

Saddleback Church has designed a unique one-year residency internship program (School of Church Leadership) for small group pastors and leaders. Residents are provided the opportunity to train and learn from Saddleback's small group team while getting hands-on ministry leadership experience.

Unique to the School of Church Leadership is the opportunity to live on our Rancho Capistrano campus. Living in community on "The Ranch" provides a way for resident interns to deepen their learning. Residents will have frequent opportunities to share ideas, empathize with common concerns, and communicate with friends and social networks. Most of all, they will explore their passion—with passion!

**Email: Director of Enlistment**
**LeadershipSchool@Saddleback.com**

 Twitter: @SB_SoCL
 Facebook: Saddleback Church School of Church Leadership

# RESOURCES from
# Saddleback and
## other leading
## small group
## ministries

At the small group
ministries website,
you'll find lots of helpful
resources.

Over 100 free down-
loadable resources

The top resources used
at Saddleback
   - to build your ministry
   - to train your leaders
   - to build health in your
      small groups

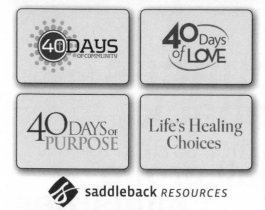